Ouija Board

A Short Guide on Safely Using Your Board

(Communicate and Harness the Power of the Great Archangels)

Rodney Risley

Published By **Cathy Nedrow**

Rodney Risley

All Rights Reserved

Ouija Board: A Short Guide on Safely Using Your Board (Communicate and Harness the Power of the Great Archangels)

ISBN 978-1-7387533-7-6

No part of this guidebook shall be reproduced in any form without permission in writing from the publisher except in the case of brief quotations embodied in critical articles or reviews.

Legal & Disclaimer

The information contained in this book is not designed to replace or take the place of any form of medicine or professional medical advice. The information in this book has been provided for educational & entertainment purposes only.

The information contained in this book has been compiled from sources deemed reliable, and it is accurate to the best of the Author's knowledge; however, the Author cannot guarantee its accuracy and validity and cannot be held liable for any errors or omissions. Changes are periodically made to this book. You must consult your doctor or get professional medical advice before using any of the suggested remedies, techniques, or information in this book.

Upon using the information contained in this book, you agree to hold harmless the Author from and against any damages, costs, and expenses, including any legal fees potentially resulting from the application of any of the information provided by this guide. This disclaimer applies to any damages or injury caused by the use and application, whether directly or indirectly, of any advice or information presented, whether for breach of contract, tort, negligence, personal injury, criminal intent, or under any other cause of action.

You agree to accept all risks of using the information presented inside this book. You need to consult a professional medical practitioner in order to ensure you are both able and healthy enough to participate in this program.

Table Of Contents

Chapter 1: History Of The Ouija Board 1

Chapter 2: The Medical Thing 13

Chapter 3: Always Address Summoned Spirits With Politeness And Recognize ... 31

Chapter 4: What If It Would Now Not Art Work? 39

Chapter 5: Meeting A Malevolent Entity 54

Chapter 6: How To Use A Ouija Board.... 60

Chapter 7: The Technological Facts In The Back Of The Ouija Board 121

Chapter 8: Real-Existence Research With The Ouija Board 132

Chapter 9: The Spiritual And Religious Components Of The Ouija Board 171

Chapter 1: History Of The Ouija Board

Before the Ouija board changed into placed on marketplace, it have been registered, and examined, inside the Patent and Trademark Office so you can be approved. Elijah J. Bond, a legal professional from Baltimore specialised in licenses, have become one of the first to deposit the patent of the Ouija on February 10th, 1891. Charles Kennard, additionally from Baltimore, delivered together four extraordinary clients to begin the Kennard Novelty Company and sell the Ouija Board to the general public. None of them have been spiritualists, nor did they ever address every different paranormal practices: they were marketers who found an unrepeatable possibility and desired to benefit from it.

It is commonly believed that, to create the call, the phrases "Oui" and "Ja" had been merged, however this is not the reality. Robert Murch, an historian of Ouija, said that, based at the research he achieved, it modified into Elijah J. Bond's sister-in-regulation, Helen Peters, who came up with an intuitive and easy to don't forget call. The creators, regardless of the reality that, claimed that it modified into the board itself that advocated the decision, which intended "Good Luck".

Newspapers from 1981 advertised it with the headline "Ouija, the tremendous talking board", bought through the usage of Pittsburgh. Pittsburgh described it as a paranormal tool that responded to questions on the beyond, gift and future with great precision; an device halfway maximum of the regarded and the unknown. The company promised in no manner ending fun for human beings of every age and bought the Ouija board for $1.50 in toy stores. It didn't encompass any instructions the least bit, it excellent said that it did what it promised, and this accelerated the halo of thriller round it and intrigued humans even extra.

Ouija boards haven't changed an lousy lot with time regardless of the reality that a few have introduced phrases or symbols, together with exclamation or query marks. The first Ouija forums had been made out of wood, however these days further they may be comprised of plastic, resin or cardboard.

As we will see, the cause modified into that of a smooth board sport with which one may need to spend time within the business enterprise of friends and, on the same time, it have end up furthermore marketed as a paranormal oracle.

The initial concept come to be that or more humans, sitting on contrary sides, would likely region their fingertips on the planchette, a small tear-formed device, after which proceeded to ask questions and checked out the solutions indicated with the aid of way of the pointer.

Mediums, earlier than others, detested the Ouija boards due to the reality their paintings have become undermined with the useful resource of this new tool.

In 1892, the Kennard Novelty Company elevated with the aid of getting factories in Baltimore, in New York, in Chicago and one in London.

The following three hundred and sixty five days, Kennard and Bond had been no longer part of the industrial enterprise corporation, and William Fuld, from smooth worker and shareholder, commenced out dealing with the enterprise.

In the twelve months 1920 the Ouija board income amounted to 3 million.

Fuld then died in 1927, sufferer of a mysterious fall from the roof of a newly constructed manufacturing facility.

In 1944, manner to one of the organization's warehouses in New York, fifty thousand Ouija forums had been offered.

In 1965 the Parker Bros. Company supplied the rights of the Ouija board and the subsequent year there were million portions provided, beating the traditional board endeavor Monopoly.

Robert Murch stated that earlier than he began his studies on this tool, no character knew its origins. This surprised Murch, because it emerge as such an iconic, mysterious and curious object. Murch described: "Communicating with the dead turn out to be common, it wasn't visible as weird or bizarre. It's difficult to assume that now, we observe that and suppose, 'Why are you setting up the gates of hell?'"

At the time, nobody from the Kennard Novelty Company had any intention of starting off the gates of hell, simplest to open Americans' wallets.

In 1848 America have emerge as almost passionate about spiritualism, thanks in difficulty to the Fox sisters, who publicly claimed to get keep of messages from spirits, that is why the Ouija board determined fertile ground to flourish once it emerge as placed in the market thru the Kennard Novelty Company years later. Almost each family within the United States had a Ouija board hidden inside the house, or perhaps leaning in sight, type of like a few special normal piece of furniture.

In the second one half of of of the nineteenth Century, the adherents of spiritualism numbered inside the tens of thousands and thousands: it turned into compatible with Christian dogma so there has been no fear of inciting the divine wrath. Not fine have emerge as the Ouija board well-known, however moreover emerge as computerized writing and all the precise mediumistic techniques which incorporates table turning séances.

Mary Todd Lincoln, partner of President Abraham Lincoln, held séances in the White House while her eleven-year-antique son died of fever in 1862. During the American Civil War the adherents to those practices multiplied even greater, they favored to try to talk with their sons and husbands that perished or disappeared in battle.

I dare to say that that is a fantastic clarification as to why there were so many instances of possessions, poltergeists and hauntings, if we look at the documented ones. All folks who wished to speak with the deceased by no means paid hobby to the truth that they had to protect themselves or to purify their homes after the séances.

Brandon Hodge, historian of spiritism, asserted that there has been lots frustration from humans in search of to get one single big message from the spirits. Waiting for the spirit to run through the complete the board and the letters, earlier than stopping on one, have turn out to be tedious. Hodge puzzled why the spirits have been now not capable of communicate quicker with the telegraph, which had already been in trade for many years. "Why are they so tough to achieve?", he puzzled.

Over the years there were many tales that seemed inside the newspapers which noticed Ouija forums featured as protagonists. One instance is one article of the New York Times posted in 1920, it stated a Chicago girl who ended up in a psychiatric medical institution because of the fact the spirits told her to depart the corpse of her mom in the dwelling room for fifteen days in advance than burying her inside the out of doors.

In 1916, Pearl Curran claimed that the poems she had written had been dictated to her via the Ouija board by means of manner of the usage of the spirit of Patience Worth, who died inside the seventeenth century. A year later, Emily Grant Hutchings, Pearl

Curran's friend, had a comparable story at the aspect of her e-book "Jap Herron".

Pulitzer prize-prevailing poet James Merrill, along together together with his epic poem known as "The Changing Light at Sandover", stimulated with the useful resource of using the Ouija, gained the National Book Critics Circle Award in 1982. Merrill stated that the spirit board have become useful to him as a manner of introspection, in desire to as a device to talk with the deceased.

The film "The Exorcist", inspired by the usage of way of actual sports, added a current-day and dark slight at the Ouija board due to the truth the primary person Regan were possessed thru a Demon after gambling with the mediumistic device that regarded simplest for a few moments in the movie version through the use of William Peter Blatty. After that movie, the idea about the Ouija board had modified deeply in people, primary them to simply accept as true with that it changed right into a demonic device.

From that second on, those who offered the forums, now not did so for non secular or leisure reasons but, as a substitute, to undertaking right into a present day and unknown danger.

Many spiritual corporations recognized the Ouija board as Satan's desired approach of conversation, and in 2001 in Alamogordo, New Mexico, a Ouija board modified into burned collectively with copies of Disney's Snow White movie and some Harry Potter books.

Pat Robertson, seven hundred Club's host[2], in 2011 said that Demons can acquire us via the board.

When Murch began to speak approximately the tool at a paranormal convention, he was interrupted for the motive that the mission scared people too much.

Recently, this tool has regained reputation way to the many movies and Hasbro, no longer Parker Brothers, has advertised a greater vital version than the primary crimson colored one, promoting the rights to a secondary enterprise that would maintain producing them devoted to the originals.

Hasbro has renamed the planchette as "message indicator".

In present day years, but no longer most effective, many movies were shot and severa novels were written in which Ouija forums are gift, regardless of the truth that no longer they all are to be taken as appropriate material to check on. Here are some:

Movies

Spiritica/ Witchboard (UK/ USA) – 1986

Ouija (Spain) – 2003

Bunshinsaba (South Korea) – 2004

Séance (USA) – 2006

Satanic (USA) – 2006

Ouija/ Séance (Philippines) – 2007

Greetings (UK) – 2007

The Unleashed (Canada) – 2011

Séance: The Summoning (USA) – 2011

Books

Ouija: A Dead Oaks Terrors Series Novel (Rena Marin; Skylar McKinzie) – 2019 (USA)

Jap Herron: A Novel Written From the Ouija Board (Emily Grant Hutchings) – 1917 (USA)

Human Ouija (L. Bachman) – 2016 (USA)

La Tavola Ouija (Gregorio Prestifilippo) – 2016 (Italy)

Chapter 2: The Medical Thing

Science has already spoken out approximately Ouija boards, citing that they do not virtually help in contacting entities. Scientists reiterate that Ouija boards paintings way to a principle that has been diagnosed for over one hundred sixty years referred to as the Ideomotor phenomenon, which means that that it's the person, unconsciously, who actions the planchette with out figuring out it.

William Benjamin Carpenter end up a physiologist and clinical health practitioner, and in 1852 he published a record for the Royal Institutional of Great Britain that examined automatic muscle actions that rise up without aware will, which includes the act of crying even as searching a dramatic movie. It become putting to have a observe that this phenomenon is likewise reproduced at the same time as the usage of this sort of forums.

In 1853 Michael Faraday[3], a chemist and physicist, conducted a series of desk-turning experiments, displaying that their motion become because of the Ideomotor actions of the humans. However, no longer in all instances there has been an Ideomotor Phenomenon.

Dr. Charles French[4], psychology professor at Goldsmiths University, London, stated: "It can generate a totally robust have an impact on that the movement is being due to some outdoor employer, but it's no longer. Dowsing rods, Oujia boards, pendulums, small tables, they're all devices wherein a quite a small muscular motion can cause pretty a large effect."

Automatic writing or maybe the fake bomb detection kits that fooled dozens of global governments artwork within the identical way.

Many of the primary planchettes had been organized with small wheels, designed to facilitate motion on the floor underneath.

In order to take part in a session, you abandon your aware control due to the fact you decided "I am no longer the one who actions it" and, via doing so, you persuade yourself of this permitting the hand and arm to be encouraged via the usage of way of the unconscious. Even believing that the desk is endowed with mystical forces allows to give up to as a minimum one's inner impulses.

It is sufficient to anticipate that every day we carry out aware and unconscious actions. For instance, if you want to eat, you enhance your arm voluntarily and also you supply the fork to the mouth whilst the eye closes the eyelid without you giving the conscious command to perform that.

There had been mentalists who, on level, have delivered a Ouija board as a stunt to carry out thru calling human beings within the target market to participate in a séance, satisfied that the planchette come to be sliding at the board way to involuntary actions. The mentalists might also want to ask a few questions that the participants knew the solution to and, the board, through the humans, responded correctly.[5]

In case the mind doesn't understand the answer, it's going to waft the arm towards the most cheap answer dictated with the beneficial useful resource of the subconscious.

In this regard, a bit of writing posted in Vox places it this manner:

"Your mind can subconsciously create photos and reminiscences whilst you ask inquiries to the board. The frame responds to the mind without you "forcing" it to achieve this consciously, in order that the muscle companies of the hands and hands flow the pointer to the responses which you, again subconsciously, might also want to receive.

And proper proper right here's wherein things get really interesting:

Over the years, studies has determined that the Ideomotor phenomenon is carefully associated with unconscious recognition and that its impact is maximized at the same time as the concern believes she or he has no manipulate over his actions. Paradoxically, the lots a good deal much less manipulate you trust you studied you've got have been given, the extra your subconscious thoughts is exercise it as an possibility.

This is wherein the triangular pointer of the Ouija board performs its issue in the sport. The planchette simplifies the unconscious manage of muscle moves because it concentrates and directs them, even if you suppose you do not have control over them.

It is also the purpose why the planchette appears to transport even extra effectively whilst more human beings use it concurrently: it frees really absolutely everyone's mind via permitting them to subconsciously generate the worrying solutions of the Ouija board."

Vox gives, as I did, that still different apparent paranormal activities are trouble to the Ideomotor phenomenon: automated writing, demonic ownership, dowsing and so on. This effect has additionally been the idea of diverse hoaxes, frauds and scams over the years.

To make sure that you are not talking for your unconscious, all you want to do is to blindfold yourself and to tape the whole thing with a video camera or via way of getting an external man or woman to look at the state of affairs. Participants have to no longer look at the board, nor recognise who has the Ouija board coping with them, in any other case the thoughts can unconsciously memorize the position of the letters and flow the arm because of this. This is due to the fact everything we see, even in a distracted way, is memorized without us being aware of it, and even if the thoughts forgets, the whole lot may be recovered through meditation or regressive hypnosis.

False myths to debunk

On the internet there are many rumors, platitudes, commonplaces and pretend beliefs designed, for the maximum detail, to frighten or to arouse hobby approximately the difficult to understand. The first ones come from Christian hand, which may be looking for to distance, specially more younger people, from the so-called "evil". The latter are written, for maximum of the times, by using bloggers or writers searching out some clean visibility. In most in their writings there can be a not unusual warning: do not use it and, even, no longer to very very own one at domestic.

I do no longer assume that, whoever claims this, has ever achieved a séance. But, you comprehend, workout brings experience, and revel in brings expertise.

Below is a list of the diverse myths that flow into spherical the problem and, with you, I will speak what's actual and what isn't always.

Don't use the Ouija board due to the truth you can fall victim to a demonic possession.

False.

This is instead now not likely. To be a victim of a possession one should have a completely susceptible air of mystery, low power and want a deep purification of the complete religious and cloth frame.

Moreover, Demons could not benefit some factor from taking ownership of a human frame, but ought to handiest accomplish that if invited thru an invocation.

Who should purpose a possession is as a substitute the spirit of a deceased, because of the fact, trapped in limbo (this size however without a body), can undergo the loneliness and anger of having nobody to speak with. In most instances a spirit can see people, despite the fact that he is aware about that they will by no means see him. This causes robust feelings to grant it the energy to take ownership of a person with low defenses. First, the spirit will discover trouble in studying a frame of physical strength, that's why we are capable of see it waft in a mechanical, discombobulated manner and it's going to have a guttural voice. In this sort of case I do now not advise contacting an exorcist because he might also want to pleasant torture the unlucky psychologically and bodily. There exist painless rituals each for the person and for the spirit which, in this situation, must not be demonized however helped due to the fact that is a determined try to be heard and aided.

Do now not try to burn the Ouija board to damage it: it will scream and actually every person who hears that scream will die inner thirty-six hours.

Burning the Ouija board does no longer please the spirits and it is not truely beneficial to perform that. There is a possibility that they may get indignant, they may purpose problems, and there may be a much off and small faraway danger that they will appear their anger via this method, mainly with the most used forums. However, even though there were screams or wonderful paranormal activities in a few unspecified time inside the future of the burning of the board, no one might die.

Never ask on what day or which manner you may die.

Knowing the date of your dying is a exquisite responsibility. It is obvious that folks that are aware of it will strive a few thing, on that day, to avoid it. But what if it's exactly in an try to keep away from lack of lifestyles that the prediction comes actual? Let me deliver an reason for higher with an example:

Giovanna is privy to that these days she ought to die. But she would possibly now not need to die, so she remains at home all day and she or he or he or he pretends to be unwell to no longer go to work, glad that she can escape all chance. Yet, as she walks throughout the house, her cat runs amongst her legs, inflicting her to stumble and provide manner, hitting her head on the point of the table. If Giovanna hadn't diagnosed the date of her loss of lifestyles and went to paintings, the cat would possibly by no means have introduced approximately her to stumble and as a cease end result die.

However, many spirits need to deceive and consequently, via the usage of using requesting the day of your loss of life, they could come up with a random date handiest for the amusing of searching you pass crazy until the given day.

Don't ask for a sign of its presence, you may only get your self into trouble; besides, the spirit you are in conversation with isn't always able to it.

Partially real. Not all spirits and entities very own enough power to transport devices or reason noise.

Once, at the same time as appearing a séance, one of the participants requested the spirit if it could bypass an item. The response grow to be, "I am not a clown." You can brush aside the relaxation of its declaration.

Never ask questions on God.

Saying "God" can be misunderstood. There are not any Gods inside the astral realm, however more or less effective entities, of better or decrease degree, vibrating at better or decrease frequencies. There are the ones ruling over exclusive spirits, but, there isn't always one above or underneath all others. It's form of like asking which one is the person that "is in price" of all companies at some point of the planet.

If we are speaking about "Source", it's each special rely. It is stated that all souls come from the One, from the common Source, that is an agglomeration of energies able to developing new spirits. It has no recognition, we ought to nearly look at it to an power reserve.

Do now not allow supernatural forces to depend variety the numbers or undergo the alphabet in a decreasing experience, within the occasion that they succeed they will escape from the Ouija board.

The Ouija board is not a room in which you lock up spirits. By starting a séance, the responding spirit stays certain to it until you close it (push aside the entity). Nothing more.

During my first revel in the entity had lengthy beyond numerous times via the numbers and the letters in each one direction and the opportunity, earlier than mission a nice conversation.

Make the planchette pass across the board in circles as regularly due to the fact the variety because the participants of the séance.

There is not any real motive to do that, if not to fee it. I did it myself as soon as I did no longer get any response and, in fact, then they replied. There are, but, distinct methods for charging the Ouija in conjunction with setting lit candles, in semi-darkness, above or on the fringe of the board. It additionally can be finished with the imposition of palms or via using putting a copper pyramid on top of it, in case you rise up to have one.

Never use a Ouija board in places wherein spirits can accumulate, which embody cemeteries, haunted houses and wherein tragedies have occurred.

I as quickly as examine this sentence, concerning the spirits in a cemetery: If I have been to die and grow to be a spirit, I must no longer want to be wherein my corpse is. It is much more likely that the spirit of a deceased character remains in the place in which he or she died, in place of living in a cemetery. Regardless, this word is a super caution. Where murders and tragedies have taken region there's going to be greater power there than anywhere else, and therefore contacts are maximum favorable, in particular with any larvae that can be present there to feed upon the energies of that area.

Never use a Ouija board by myself.

To make such an item art work, the power of , 3 or extra human beings is wanted. Who is an expert in Esotericism or Spiritism discourages the usage of the board through a unmarried character handiest for the dearth of sufficient energies to properly use it. Otherwise it stays an incredible device to talk together with your non-public unconscious.

Many superior esotericists, however, love to use it in solitude to contact their Spirit Guides.

On the alternative, the danger does not will growth if it's miles first-class one individual to use the board, however instead, if there are several people to open the portal, then larvae are more likely to be extra attracted to the séance.

To guard you from spirits, visualize round your frame a white mild.

Great advice! Before appearing a séance, I advise you to visualize (recall) a colourful white or blue slight around your frame, on the equal time as repeating for your thoughts: "This light protects me from everything that is horrible for me".

To see the entity you're communicating with, look through the lens related to the planchette.

False and unfounded assertion, with all opportunity born from some films that have been made approximately it.

If the planchette time and again suggests the widespread variety eight, it way it's miles managed through an evil spirit.

During a séance, the spirit with whom we were in touch become constantly writing "666", claiming to be a demon and looking to kick us out of the location that he claimed as his very very own. I immediately discovered out his deception, and informed him that he come to be now not the demon he claimed to be, however best a spirit asking to be left in peace.

He then confirmed my accusation. Next, he made a few bricks fall from the ceiling which fell at the ground approximately three toes from us, as a warning[6].

By this I recommend to mention that the spirits and entities that we contact can lie, pretend to be who they may be no longer, that lets in you to spook us.

As for the above statement, there's no practical motive for it to be actual.

If an evil spirit were to hang-out the Ouija board use the pointer (or lens) the alternative manner up.

Again, there are no valid or vast motives to justify this, nor can I find out a reasonable explanation.

Chapter 3: Always Address Summoned Spirits With Politeness And Recognize

I would possibly classify this due to the fact the equal antique to usually observe, whether or not one have been to encounter an evil spirit, similarly to a extremely good one.

Faq

Is this a satanic device?

No.

Why have to it's?

You do now not just meet Demons[7], but moreover Angels and spirits of the departed. In maximum of my critiques I virtually have met my Spirit Guides, who in truth are Demons. They have constantly been very well mannered and type, they furnished me with the solutions I needed and when they even located time to comedian story round a chunk.

Is it unstable?

It relies upon on how you operate it. It's unstable in case you carry out a séance out of mere interest, as a endeavor, at the same time as you're being disrespectful or if you use it to kill time due to boredom. We additionally run into danger whilst we do no longer have the essential know-how to well perform a séance, guard ourselves, and beat back any unwanted traffic.

If you have to encounter a spirit of a deceased individual, and ask him questions related to his death, you could purpose emotions of anger, hatred, or worry.

When one encounters a larva, then certainly there is threat. In that case you need to in reality say thank you and close to the séance.

Once, whilst searching for to get in touch with a deceased uncle, we had a verbal exchange with a larva that have been parasitizing whom we have been looking for. It should now not allow us to talk to him, but I in a well mannered way asked to provide us virtually three questions and it agreed. Despite this, I do now not advise attempting this sort of gamble. A larva can parasitize someone without the situation being aware of it, foremost to poor emotional states, inflicting pain and plenty of different sorrows. In truth, you may enchantment to a larva truely because of the truth you do not perform a regular active cleaning of your own home and yourself.

You want to keep your Ouija board a long way from children as they will be the favorite prey of larvae and Energy Vampires.

The viable dangers aren't confined to parasitic entities, however also to those spirits who respond with lies.

However, if one does have a Spirit Guide, this one also can need to intervene and help the person of the board.

What if I stumble upon a horrible entity?

First and main, don't go away the consultation and do not be disrespectful. Explain to the negative entity the manner you experience, irrespective of only a few phrases; as an instance, "I don't suppose you may be of any help to us, we thank you except and we near the séance." Then, lead the planchette over to "Goodbye", cleanse the residence and all the folks that attended the séance.

Do I need to purify the Ouija?

Yes. I propose doing this as speedy as you get it home, whether or not it is already been used or no longer. To do so you can use shamanic sage or palo santo and ensure the smoke gets to touch it everywhere. Another manner is to location your Ouija board on top of a platter full of salt for 3 days and 3 nights.

You should moreover do that at the surrender of every consultation, mainly when you have encountered any larvae or one of a kind malignant entities.

Do I need to burn it?

No.

There are movies and novels that speak about burning the board to kill any "Demons" trapped in it, despite the fact that that is impossible. If the séance wasn't concluded in the suitable way, the spirit ought to grow to be linked to the board, and it absolutely may now not please him. To get spherical this, certainly open a ultra-modern session, say thanks and near it by way of way of predominant the planchette over "Goodbye".

Burning a Ouija board is disrespectful and perilous.

I can't hold it inside the residence, so in which?

In case you do now not use the Ouija, it'll continue to be much like each one-of-a-kind piece of family furnishings, you can bear in thoughts it to be the same of an vintage unused mobile phone. We ought to do the equal reasoning with a pen, for the motive that it can be used for automatic writing or a pendulum, because it lets in us to touch the spirits and communicate with them.

Where can I get one?

There are many on-line stores that promote them. For some time, my companion and I made severa of them, some of that have been furthermore asked through an esoteric strong factor keep that also has a small ebook vicinity on the problem indoors. It takes place often that we get commissioned to make a few Ouija boards, and now we simplest motive them to on request.

It occurs, however, to not be capable of provide you with the money for one, so I propose you're making one yourself the use of just a few things. You will need a sheet of paper, a pen and a glass cup, or likely a coin, so as to feature as a planchette.

Warning: if the piece of paper or the board receives broken, then the entities might not respond.

You can use any material to make it, be it timber or even plastic, regardless of the truth that you have to prefer to use most effective natural materials.

When you create a few thing you establish an invisible link with the item, this lets in it to feature better with you in place of with each person else.

I do no longer recognize any medium, how can I do that?

You do now not want a medium, however as an alternative a person who's capable of lead and manage a séance with out being traumatic if the flame of the candle wavers or if there are noises in the environment. I specify this because of the truth someone recommended to me that they have deserted using the board exactly due to the fact a few trouble paranormal came about, as a end end result exactly what is supposed to occur.

In order to have a extra possibility of touch, it's miles quality to carry out the séance in three or four people for a clean depend of being capable of channel the sufficient amount of electricity required to carry out the consultation.

Chapter 4: What If It Would Now Not Art Work?

No problem. Simply say thanks and near the session as you'll within the occasion that that they had answered. I realize a few people do not do that after which fail to understand that the subsequent troubles that arise to them are precisely due to the lack of a right closure of the séance.

The factors at the back of a lack of reaction, but, may be numerous: you're doing all of your séance in a place wherein there aren't any entities, the spirits in attendance are not inquisitive about answering your call, the attendees do not possess sufficient strength to initiate communication and to assist the entity go with the flow the planchette, the Ouija board is broken, the planchette does now not slide effortlessly for the duration of the board.

What no longer to do at the identical time as appearing a séance

None of the attendees should partecipate to the séance if they're feeling tired, indignant, or traumatic.

None of the those who're afraid want to enroll in the consultation.

Never disrespect whoever/a few aspect solutions the decision, although they display as lots as be terrible entities.

Do not ask for the spirit to manifest, which incorporates asking to transport devices or to make noises. At maximum, you may ask it to wave the flame of the candle.

Don't believe all the topics the spirits say. Sometimes they opt to mislead and to faux to be whom they'll be now not.

Do not use or maintain your cellular mobile cellphone, or every other virtual gadgets, for your pocket further to shut to the Ouija board.

Don't ask trivial or silly questions.

Don't tease the spirits.

Don't freak out whilst the planchette movements; stay calm and manage your emotions. Larvae are inquisitive about horrible energies and fear produces exactly that.

Never circulate your palms or legs: doing so does not permit your energies to drift properly.

If larvae or specific malignant entities display up, thank them and close to the séance. Afterward you have to cleanse the board, the house, yourself and the alternative people of the session in the event that they do not recognize a way to do it themselves.

If the spirits are being rude and taunting ask them with politeness to forestall.

During the séance, do not rise up or leave the desk.

Do now not placed on necklaces, bracelets or one-of-a-type metallic devices: it interferes with the conversation.

At the quit of the session explicit your gratitude, even if you did no longer get a reaction, and then disregard the spirit via principal the pointer over to Goodbye.

What to do within the direction of a séance

When you begin, ask smooth questions whose solution need to be "Yes" or "No." Do no longer explicit your self too speedy, nor ask more than one question at the equal time. Ask one problem, look ahead to the spirit to respond and then for it to complete. You can also inform it has finished answering even as the planchette wanders lazily approximately the board with out a vacation spot.

Be patient due to the reality the entities do no longer always reply at once, they will even go with the flow the pointer apparently for no obvious reason: they're familiarizing with the board.

Only use the Ouija board if you have all the important statistics to gather this. You need to understand the way to both purify and protect your self.

Cleanse the board and the venue earlier than you start the séance. Also moderate a few white candles and an incense.

Keep the room dimly lit preferring the light from candle flames over artificial lighting.

Chat with each entity whilst preserving a deferential and friendly attitude, not servile. Treating them as pals is exceptional.

Make sure the vicinity in that you are going to hold your séance is quiet. You need to keep away from any disturbance and you should not interrupt the séance before dismissing the spirits and last the connection. Avoid crowded or noisy places.

Always near the séance at the same time as you are done, most essential the planchette on the word Goodbye after you have got got expressed your gratitude.

Protection earlier than the séance

Although coping with real dangers with the Ouija board is hard, I even though advise to protect your self earlier than you carry out any operation with it. There are many techniques, from the simplest to the most superior, and you can pick in keeping with the time at your disposal and on your records on the esoteric scenario. What I will percentage with you presently are protection strategies that you could use usually, and not truely for the use of the spirit board.

Hyaline Crystal

Also called cristallo di Rocca and Hyaline Quartz. You can located on one round your neck or maybe keep it your pocket but to gain greater advantage from it it's miles maximum suitable to cleanse and fee it first. Amethyst is likewise an tremendous first-class friend for protection.

Lavender

Hang lavender sachets throughout the room or convey one for your pocket. Every complete moon they need to all be uncovered to moonlight which will price them.

Energy sphere

Certainly no longer each person is able to do it, but I'll factor out it besides in case you can already be capable of do it or if you may be in the destiny. Close your eyes and loosen up. Take long, deep breaths. Visualize a waterfall of moderate falling from the Heavens enveloping you, infusing you with protecting energy. Bring your hands ahead, hands going via every exquisite, and create interior of them a luminous sphere, redirecting the strength that honestly replenished you. When you are completed, form it to resemble a glowing "bubble" all round you, whilst repeating the ones phrases: "This electricity protects me from the whole thing this is terrible for me".

Cleansing

Salt

Take a bowl, ideally made from glass, and placed a few salt at the bottom. Lay a chunk of cloth on pinnacle of the salt, some paper tissue will do the trick honestly as well. This will keep the stone from corroding after it comes into contact with the salt. Take the item you want to cleanse, in this situation the crystal, and place it on the material. Don't touch it for 3 days and three nights. To eliminate the salt, you may certainly dissolve it under water to your kitchen sink.

Water

Take your crystal and place it under taking walks water. Visualize all of the bad energies, black and heavy, flowing down way to the water and then visualize a vibrant and smooth electricity taking their area. Pay interest to water-soluble stones.

Laying on of palms

This one is extra advanced. Hold the crystal for your palms or lay your palms some inches above it. Close your eyes and lighten up. Visualize a amazing white power coming out of your hand chakras to fill the stone, converting the black strength that turn out to be previously permeating it.

Charging

Fire

Take the crystal and area 4 candles on each of its facets. It want to simplest be their mild to light up it. Leave it there for a few hours. If you are the use of Tea Lights, they need to honestly burn out.

Tree

Lay the stone over the roots of a big tree or, ideally, bury it in their region. The older the tree, the greater it'll price it.

Imposition of arms

With the equal function as earlier than, as soon as I spoke to you approximately the laying on of hands, visualize an intense and colourful azure power that permeates the stone and even as doing so deliver it the purpose to be useful in protective you.

Who you could touch?

Many specific forms of entities may be encountered at some point of séances. Like us, they own a massive type of personalities and inclinations. Most of the time we come upon spirits with low vibrational levels, but it's far not all of them. Some want to talk some element to us, others are truly curious about the choice. What follows isn't always a manual, however as an alternative only warning signs and symptoms.

Mischievous/playful spirits

Many spirits experience supplying phony, reputedly nonsensical solutions, or answering in languages we do not know. Sometimes, they'll cover objects. In this situation, civilly ask them to reply in a manner that you could apprehend and to supply a few problem they have got moved again to its rightful region due to the reality you are currently bored with playing.

Spirit Guides

Very frequently one's Spirit Guides or Guardians can also moreover come. They respond cordially and might put off doubts or help us in our spiritual ascension. If one encounters evil entities and spirits, it isn't uncommon for the ones Guides to interfere to help their "protégés".

Larvae

These are risky entities that I truly have treated earlier than. They can answer questions but aren't constantly inclined to perform that. They feed on human beings's power and can even latch on to someone. That is why you must now not be afraid at some stage in a séance, otherwise you might risk attracting one. They can reason accidents and depart visible marks at the frame at the facet of scratches, cuts, burns and so forth.

Once, inside the course of a session, we were seeking to touch the spirit of a deceased person, however it couldn't respond to us due to the reality a larva prevented it from doing so, feeding on its electricity. By bargaining with the larva, I controlled to get it to permit us to invite the spirit most effective 3 questions. All taken into consideration, this larva modified into type to us as it already had its prey to feed on, but regardless of my verbal attempts to get it away from the deceased, there has been no manner I have to get it to be aware of me. I need to have done so in one in all a type approaches, however, it became now not my reason and, as an earthly soul, I must best address topics related to this fabric size.

Demons

Contrary to well-known notion, speakme with a Demon is not an unpleasant event, quite the alternative! Demons belong to the Goetic Pantheon, that is the handiest described in Solomon's texts. This Pantheon includes seventy-two entities which were previously part of extremely good Pagan Pantheons and have been given "accumulated" together proper into a first rate one. The same Isis, the Egyptian Deity, is a Demon known as Astaroth, a Deity of love, and is also called Ishtar, Sumerian. Marduk is Babylonian while Beelzebub is also Sumerian. There isn't always anything scary approximately those Deities besides for the picture that Christianity imposed over them. Ultimately, to say to have talked with Horus, the half of-hawk Egyptian God, is like saying that you spoke with a Demon.

There is one element to component out: they're kind to people who deal with them with recognize inside the identical way as every other entity. I endorse, if you insult someone you do now not recognise simply because of the truth a person stated: "That person is awful", they will in no manner be extremely good to you. I want to remind you that a few entities make the maximum famous beliefs and faux to be Demons a awesome way to purpose fright to others, so do no longer worry a Demon if it gives itself, but be cautious top notch of the spirits that offer you with purpose to expect which is probably evil.

Thought paperwork

This is not an real entity however an Egregore: condensed strength that can have obtained a existence of its own. They may be created consciously or unconsciously. In this second case, if you have a morbid and fixed thought approximately a few trouble, a Thought Form may be created, that is because of the fact concept is power. They can frequently turn out to be larvae to live on and may be risky to people who come in touch with them. A genuine reason for the well-known Mystical Marian visions need to exactly be that they'll be Thought Forms. Imagine hundreds or hundreds of human beings concentrating their prayers on a unmarried focal issue: the Madonna. All of this strength is directed within the path of the same purpose whether or now not or no longer one prays to Our Lady of Lourdes, the Black Madonna or Our Lady of Guadalupe for they'll be representations of the equal parent.

Chapter 5: Meeting A Malevolent Entity

It might also additionally moreover display up, within the direction of a consultation, to come across entities that are not within the least quality. There are many purple flags to which one should be privy to, although it's no longer continuously smooth to apprehend the actual nature of a spirit due to the reality they're able to lie or faux to be first-class if you want to collect their functions. Read this carefully and memorize it: If you stumble upon any of those warnings symptoms, you may maximum possibly must terminate the séance.

The spirit scoffs, insults, or mocks one or greater participants in the consultation;

The spirit claims to be "evil" or to need to harm a person;

The spirit lies;

The spirit offers itself as a Demon or writes "666" on the board (nearly virtually it's achieved to scare you and no longer because it surely has some element to do with Satan).

If you word any of the behaviors listed above, or others which may be troubling you, you can really ask for a trade in thoughts-set. If the spirit writes in a language that you don't understand, you may ask it to talk in a manner that you could recognize. If you want to maintain the consultation, but with out that precise entity, ask them in a well mannered way to move away. The following phrase may go: "Please, I ask you to step decrease lower back and allow someone else respond. I thanks to your responses."

Other uses of the ouija board

Pendulum and Ouija

There are many boards within the market with letters and numbers written in a circle; those are notable for using the pendulum. Just relax and unfastened your thoughts, deliver the pendulum over the Ouija board simply so it swings a few centimeters from it and ask your questions. Doing so will can help you get more entire solutions than the smooth "Yes", "No" and "Maybe" of the pendulum. Don't do the pushing yourself, as it's meant to transport on its private. Furthermore, you could use it without trouble with the aid of your self.

Planchette and pencil

In the past there used to furthermore be big planchettes prepared with 3 wheels on the lowest and a hole inside the middle massive enough to preserve a pencil. After setting it on a sheet of paper, the attendees might then lay their arms at the pointer and might ask questions like they might have executed with a Ouija board. This approach may be very much like automatic writing and can, however now not continuously, require more than one man or woman.

Summoning board

You can use a Ouija board to touch a selected spirit if you comprehend its name or its sigil. All you want to do is call out to him and area the symbol below the board, but wonderful entities may additionally moreover come as nicely.

For some time, my accomplice and I made some summoning forums devoted to as a minimum one single entity every. Thanks to the ones, it's possible to talk simplest with whom you choice to speak to, however, we not often used them. It's now not smart to problem an entity for superficial reasons, therefore we then opted not to provide them similarly and to interest on making most effective the traditional spirit board.

How to open a séance

Before starting the séance you need to first cleanse the vicinity in which you'll be the usage of your Ouija board and, possibly, the board itself. Everything which you need to do have to be accomplished with utmost recognize. Place the board on a flat ground and slide the planchette over the ground to ensure it glides resultseasily. Light a few candles, preferably white, and a few notable incense. Sit surely and clean your thoughts.

When you feel ready, gently region a finger at the planchette, ideally the usage of your dominant hand, and open the séance by using using pronouncing those terms:

"I respectfully open the portal,

I ask you to answer in a cordial manner.

I promise no longer to disturb,

and on the equal time as the time comes I shall take my go away"[8]

I additionally advocate an opportunity phrase this is very much like the handiest mentioned above but in spite of the fact that legitimate:

"I respectfully open the portal,

I ask you to reply in a cordial way.

I promise now not to disturb,

and even as the time comes I will will let you circulate."

I modified the very last verse due to the fact while the spirit responds it can't always go away the session besides it's left out and this small trade is probably favored by using manner of the usage of the entities.

Chapter 6: How To Use A Ouija Board

Before the usage of a Ouija board, it is critical to understand the way it works and the right steps for using it appropriately and correctly. While a few human beings also can view the board as a smooth parlor sport, others trust that it could be a powerful tool for speaking with the lifeless or exploring the supernatural.

In this economic smash, we're going to take a more in-depth have a study how to use a Ouija board. We'll cowl the primary steps for installing the board, selecting a associate, and starting up communication with the spirits. We'll additionally communicate some of the potential risks and pitfalls of the usage of the board, and offer hints for staying stable and shielding yourself from negative energies or entities.

Whether you're a curious amateur or an skilled purchaser, this monetary catastrophe will offer you with the records and tools you need to apply a Ouija board with self perception and care. So take keep of your board, collect your buddies, and get equipped to discover the mysterious and fascinating international of the Ouija board.

Step-thru-step instructions on the way to apply a Ouija board

-Choose a quiet, dimly lit room on your session. Turn off any electronics or distractions, which consist of telephones or televisions.

-Gather your materials. You'll need a Ouija board, a planchette (the small, coronary coronary heart-normal piece that movements throughout the board), and as a minimum one associate to apply the board with.

-Decide on your goal for the consultation. Are you attempting to find to talk with a selected spirit or entity? Or are you in truth curious to see if the board works? It's crucial to have a easy cause in advance than beginning your session.

-Sit for the duration of out of your accomplice and region the board on a flat ground amongst you. Place the planchette inside the middle of the board.

-Both you and your companion need to location your fingers lightly at the planchette. Close your eyes and take a few deep breaths to relax and interest.

-Begin via asking the board if any spirits are present and would like to speak. Wait for a response, which can also come in the shape of the planchette transferring on its very private or spelling out phrases.

-Once you have got got set up communication with a spirit, ask questions and live up for a reaction. Remember to live respectful and courteous, and avoid asking non-public or invasive questions.

-If you sense uncomfortable or uneasy at any factor ultimately of the consultation, right away forestall the consultation and say good-bye to the spirit.

-When you are geared up to stop the consultation, say good-bye to the spirit and bypass the planchette to "Goodbye" at the board. Thank the spirit for speaking with you and prevent the consultation with a prayer or exceptional affirmation.

It's critical to study that using a Ouija board may be a powerful and doubtlessly volatile revel in. It's essential to method the board with recognize and caution, and to guard yourself from horrible energies or entities. Always forestall the consultation with a immoderate satisfactory purpose and say good-bye to any spirits you've got got got communicated with.

Precautions to take before the use of a Ouija board

Know your cause:

Knowing your purpose in advance than using a Ouija board is crucial for developing a tremendous and stable experience. Before the use of the Ouija board, it's vital to understand why you need to speak with spirits and what you wish to enjoy the session.

-Set your reason: Before beginning the consultation, set your purpose for using the Ouija board. Ask your self why you need to talk with spirits and what you preference to accumulate from the session.

-Identify your motivation: Ask yourself what motivates you to apply the Ouija board. Are you seeking out steerage, closure, or genuinely a connection to the religious global? Understanding your motivation will let you stay focused at a few level inside the consultation.

-Be clear for your boundaries: It's critical to set clean barriers in advance than using the Ouija board. This includes figuring out which varieties of spirits you're willing to talk with and what topics are off-limits. Setting clear obstacles can assist shield you from terrible or risky energies.

-Visualize brilliant results: Visualize fantastic results for the session, which incorporates receiving guidance, recovery, or closure. By specializing in effective results, you may sell a remarkable and peaceful environment for verbal exchange.

-Respect the approach: Remember to recognize the device and keep away from forcing conversation. It's critical to permit spirits to speak at their personal pace and to be patient and respectful within the route of the session.

Knowing your cause earlier than the usage of a Ouija board assist you to stay focused and create a powerful and constant experience. By setting easy intentions, figuring out your motivation, and visualizing extraordinary results, you may promote amazing strength and beautify your conversation with spirits.

Write down your intentions:

Writing down your intentions earlier than the usage of a Ouija board will let you stay targeted and maintain a powerful and steady surroundings for communique. When you write down your intentions, you create a bodily reminder of your reason and dreams for the session, in case you need to allow you to stay on direction and keep away from distractions.

Here are some suggestions on a way to put in writing down your intentions in advance than using a Ouija board:

-Be unique: When writing down your intentions, be as precise as feasible about what you preference to gain from the session. This can include the sorts of spirits you need to speak with, the subjects you need to talk about, or the precise guidance or restoration you are searching for.

-Use exquisite language: Use quality language whilst writing down your intentions. This can help promote first-rate strength and create a greater conducive environment for communique.

-Keep it easy: Keep your intentions easy and focused. Avoid trying to deal with too many topics at once, as this will make it hard to live centered and can result in confusion or frustration.

-Review and revise: Review your intentions before beginning the consultation, and make any crucial revisions or changes. This can assist make certain that your intentions are clean and aligned together collectively with your reason for the session.

-Visualize extremely good outcomes: Visualize effective outcomes as you write down your intentions. This will permit you to live targeted and promote a exceptional and non violent environment for communication.

Writing down your intentions before using a Ouija board will permit you to stay targeted, preserve a best environment for communication, and acquire your goals for the session. By being particular, the usage of high-quality language, maintaining it smooth, reviewing and revising, and visualizing incredible results, you can enhance your conversation with spirits and sell a brilliant and stable experience.

Visualize your intentions:

Visualization is a effective technique that will let you reputation your strength and intentions earlier than the usage of a Ouija board. When you visualize your intentions, you create a highbrow image of what you need to gain, that allows you to can help you arise your goals and sell amazing electricity for communication.

Here are some guidelines on the manner to visualize your intentions earlier than the use of a Ouija board:

-Relax and easy your mind: Find a quiet and non violent location in which you could loosen up and easy your mind. Take a few deep breaths and reputation on your breath to calm your thoughts and frame.

-Visualize your intentions: Close your eyes and visualize your intentions. Imagine yourself attaining your chosen final consequences, collectively with speakme with a particular spirit, receiving steering or recuperation, or gaining readability on a selected challenge count.

-Use all of your senses: Use all your senses to create a shiny and positive highbrow picture. Imagine what it seems like to advantage your selected final results, what you notice, pay attention, heady scent, and contact.

-Maintain a great thoughts-set: As you visualize your intentions, keep a terrific attitude and focus on wonderful results. Avoid terrible mind or doubts that could disrupt your power and intentions.

-Repeat powerful affirmations: Repeat excellent affirmations that useful resource your intentions, together with "I am open to high fine communication with spirits" or "I remember that I will achieve the steerage I want. »

Visualizing your intentions earlier than the usage of a Ouija board will let you consciousness your energy, show up your desires, and sell advantageous communication with spirits. By relaxing and clearing your mind, using all your senses, maintaining a nice mind-set, and repeating outstanding affirmations, you may beautify your visualization exercising and promote a satisfactory and strong enjoy.

Use outstanding language:

Using top notch language is an critical component of making prepared to apply a Ouija board. Positive language permit you to set a clear purpose for verbal exchange and promote a effective power that may enchantment to excellent spirits and messages.

Here are a few guidelines on a manner to apply excellent language earlier than using a Ouija board:

-Avoid horrific phrases: Avoid using horrific phrases or terms that would enchantment to horrible energies, together with "evil," "demon," or "damage." Instead, use tremendous words and phrases that sell love, slight, and superb communication.

-Focus on your favored final effects: Use superb language to cognizance for your selected outcome. For instance, in place of pronouncing "I do not want to speak to any bad spirits," say "I intend to speak with remarkable spirits who will bring me steering and readability. »

-Use affirmations: Use excellent affirmations to boost your intentions and sell effective strength. Some examples of affirmations you may use earlier than the use of a Ouija board consist of "I am open to splendid verbal exchange with spirits," "I receive as true with that I receives maintain of messages that serve my maximum right," or "I am surrounded through the use of love and mild. »

-Speak with conviction: When bringing up your intentions or affirmations, communicate with conviction and agree with in the electricity of your phrases. Your power and mindset can significantly have an impact at the final outcomes of your verbal exchange with spirits.

By the usage of wonderful language before the use of a Ouija board, you can set a clean goal for excellent verbal exchange and promote a secure and respectful surroundings for spirits to speak with you. Remember to continually approach the Ouija board with appreciate and motive, and to focus on effective consequences that serve your maximum precise.

Speak your intentions out loud:

Speaking your intentions out loud earlier than the use of a Ouija board may be a powerful way to set a easy purpose for powerful conversation and to promote a stable and respectful environment for spirits to speak with you. When you communicate your intentions out loud, you offer voice and electricity for your dreams, which can help to take area them greater correctly.

Here are some suggestions on how to talk your intentions out loud:

-Be clear and unique: When bringing up your intentions, be clean and unique about what you want to advantage. Avoid vague or ambiguous language that could create confusion or misinterpretation.

-Use high-quality language: As I noted earlier, using excellent language can sell a outstanding electricity and lure first-rate spirits and messages. Use splendid phrases and terms that promote love, moderate, and great communication.

-Speak with conviction and perception: When you speak your intentions out loud, talk with conviction and notion inside the power of your terms. Your power and thoughts-set can considerably affect the outcome of your conversation with spirits.

-Repeat your intentions: Repeat your intentions numerous times to enhance them and assist them sink into your subconscious mind. This assist you to stay focused and aligned together with your desired final consequences all through the Ouija board session.

Remember that talking your intentions out loud is simply one detail of on the point of use a Ouija board. It's important to take all critical precautions, collectively with choosing a safe area, the use of great affirmations, and focusing on your favored final results, to sell a steady and respectful surroundings for spirits to speak with you.

Trust the technique:

Trusting the method is an essential a part of the usage of a Ouija board efficaciously. When you trust the approach, you allow yourself to be open to the messages and insights that come through the board, without doubting or thinking their validity.

Here are some suggestions on the way to bear in thoughts the manner when using a Ouija board:

-Let cross of expectancies: When you have got were given particular expectancies about what you want to obtain or what messages you need to accumulate, you could unconsciously block the go along with the go with the flow of communique. Instead, technique the Ouija board consultation with an open thoughts and coronary coronary heart, and accept as true with that the messages you get maintain of can be to your maximum particular.

-Stay focused and focused: It's important to stay centered and centered at some point of the Ouija board session, as distractions and outside factors can interfere with the communication. Take deep breaths, lighten up your body, and easy your thoughts in advance than starting the session.

-Avoid forcing the planchette: When you try to pressure the planchette to transport in a positive path or to spell out unique terms, you could unknowingly have an effect on the messages that come via the board. Instead, allow the planchette to move freely and organically, and take delivery of as real with that the messages will come thru in their non-public manner and time.

-Validate the messages: When to procure messages thru the Ouija board, validate them by asking for rationalization or confirmation. This permit you to recognize the which means that and relevance of the messages, and construct remember in the communication manner.

Remember that trust is a key detail of powerful conversation with spirits thru the Ouija board. By letting skip of expectations, staying centered and focused, warding off forcing the planchette, and validating the messages, you could installation a robust sense of receive as proper with and openness with the spirits that come via the board.

By placing smooth intentions, you may create a focused and splendid strength to your Ouija board session. This can assist lessen the chance of horrible entities and make certain a stable and effective revel in.

Choose a safe region:

Choosing a safe place is every different critical step to take in advance than using a Ouija board.

Here are some pointers on a way to pick a safe location:

•Choose a quiet, non-public location:

Choosing a quiet and private vicinity is important on the same time as the use of a Ouija board as it creates a steady and centered surroundings for communique with spirits. Here are a few matters to bear in mind whilst selecting a vicinity:

-Avoid distractions: Choose a place that is free from distractions, which encompass loud noises, colorful lighting, or interruptions from distinct humans. This will help you preserve a easy and centered reference to the spirits that come via the board.

-Create a snug surroundings: Set up the area in a way that feels cushty and inviting to you. This can also encompass using clean lighting fixtures, comfortable seating, and soothing tune to create a non violent environment.

-Choose a private place: It's essential to select a location this is private and loose from undesirable interruptions. This will help you experience safe and strong sooner or later of the Ouija board consultation, and will permit you to recognition fully at the communique with spirits.

-Consider the power of the place: Before using a Ouija board in a specific area, it is important to bear in mind the strength of the space. Avoid using the board in places that experience bad or unsettling, as this may intervene with the communique technique.

By selecting a quiet and personal place, you can create a stable and targeted surroundings for the use of the Ouija board. This will let you set up a strong reference to the spirits that come through the board, and gather easy and full-size messages.

•Avoid public regions:

It's vital to keep away from the use of a Ouija board in public areas, as this can be distracting and potentially risky. Here are a few motives why it is great to use a Ouija board in a private area in location of a public one:

-Distractions: Public regions are frequently noisy and busy, with masses of human beings shifting round and growing distractions. This can make it hard to reputation at the verbal exchange with spirits and acquire easy messages.

-Safety worries: Using a Ouija board in a public space can trap undesirable hobby and in all likelihood motive volatile conditions. It's first rate to apply the board in a quiet and private place in that you sense safe and normal.

-Respect for others: Using a Ouija board in public areas can be disrespectful to others who might not percentage your ideals or enjoy uncomfortable with the interest. It's vital to be respectful of others and keep away from inflicting any useless pain or disturbance.

-Interference with spirits: Public regions are frequently complete of lots of power and hobby, that may intervene with the conversation with spirits. By the usage of the board in a non-public area, you could minimize out of doors interference and create a extra centered and sizeable connection with the spirits.

It's nice to apply a Ouija board in a non-public area in that you experience secure and comfortable. This will will permit you to create a peaceful and centered surroundings for communique with spirits, and collect easy and widespread messages.

•Ensure right lighting fixtures:

Proper lights is essential even as the use of a Ouija board, as it could create a relaxing and non violent surroundings and assist you popularity at the verbal exchange with spirits. Here are some tips for ensuring proper lighting whilst the use of a Ouija board:

-Use dim lights: It's brilliant to apply dim lighting whilst the usage of a Ouija board, as this can create a relaxing and calming surroundings. Avoid using vibrant overhead lights, which can be harsh and distracting.

-Use candles: Candles can provide a clean and calming mild that is perfect for using a Ouija board. They also can create a calming surroundings and assist you relax.

-Use a small lamp: If you do not need to apply candles, a small lamp with a easy, heat mild may be an amazing opportunity. Place the lamp close to the board to create a targeted and calming surroundings.

-Avoid the usage of flashlights: Flashlights can create a harsh and jarring mild that can be distracting and intervene with the communique with spirits. If you want greater mild, use a dim lamp or candles as a substitute.

-Choose a place with herbal mild: If possible, choose a place with natural mild, which encompass a room with a window. This can provide a smooth and calming light this is good for the use of a Ouija board.

Ensuring proper lighting fixtures is important while the use of a Ouija board. By using dim lights, candles, or a small lamp, you could create a calming and non violent surroundings this is conducive to conversation with spirits.

•Remove any distractions:

When the usage of a Ouija board, it's far crucial to do away with any distractions that could interfere with the communique with spirits. Here are some pointers for placing off distractions:

-Turn off digital gadgets: Electronic gadgets which encompass cellular telephones, computer structures, and televisions may be very distracting even as using a Ouija board. Turn off these devices or located them in a few other room to avoid any interruptions.

-Close doors and domestic windows: Outside noises which encompass web page traffic or barking dogs can be distracting on the same time as the usage of a Ouija board. Close doors and home home windows to reduce any outdoor noise.

-Choose a quiet time of day: Choose a time of day while the house or building is quiet and there are fewer distractions. Avoid the usage of the Ouija board within the direction of busy instances of day or at the same time as there are a whole lot of human beings round.

-Use headphones: If there are noises that cannot be prevented, which incorporates creation paintings or loud friends, don't forget using noise-cancelling headphones to block out the noise.

-Set barriers with others: If you're the use of the Ouija board with others, set boundaries in advance. Let them recognize that you need to restriction distractions and create a targeted surroundings for verbal exchange with spirits.

Removing distractions is essential at the same time as using a Ouija board. By minimizing out of doors noise and proscribing distractions from digital gadgets, you could create a non violent and targeted surroundings that is conducive to verbal exchange with spirits.

•Cleanse the distance:

Before using a Ouija board, it's miles crucial to cleanse the distance to put off any terrible strength or entities that can be present. Here are a few suggestions for cleansing the distance:

-Burn sage: Sage smudging is a famous method for cleaning a location. Light a bundle of dried sage and allow the smoke fill the room, ensuring to hobby on the corners and other regions in which terrible strength can be present.

-Use incense: Burning incense also can assist to cleanse the space. Choose a fragrance that you discover calming and moderate it before using the Ouija board.

-Ring a bell or chime: Ringing a bell or chime can assist to clean any awful electricity from the gap. Start at one surrender of the room and pass spherical the distance, ringing the bell or chime as you move.

-Use crystals: Certain crystals, which consist of black tourmaline and amethyst, are regarded for his or her cleansing houses. Place those crystals throughout the room to assist cleanse the distance.

-Play calming song: Soft, calming tune can help to create a peaceful and splendid environment, that could in turn assist to cleanse the space.

Cleansing the gap earlier than the use of a Ouija board can help to create a more terrific and centered surroundings for communique with spirits. By disposing of terrible energy and entities, you can create a safer and further comfortable vicinity on your Ouija board consultation.

•Set up a protective barrier:

In addition to cleaning the distance, putting in place a shielding barrier can assist to ensure a steady and high-quality Ouija board enjoy. Here are some pointers for putting in vicinity a shielding barrier:

-Visualize a shielding guard: Close your eyes and visualize a white or golden protective defend surrounding you and all and sundry else taking part within the Ouija board consultation. Imagine the guard as a powerful pressure if you need to hold out any awful energy or entities.

-Call on defensive spirits: You can also call on protective spirits or entities to assist installation a barrier. Some human beings like to name on angels, spirit guides, or specific extraordinary entities for protection.

-Use defensive symbols: Certain symbols, which includes the pentagram or the Eye of Horus, are believed to have protecting residences. You can draw those symbols on a chunk of paper and vicinity them on the desk in which you may be the use of the Ouija board.

-Burn shielding herbs: Burning herbs together with rosemary or lavender can help to create a protecting barrier round the distance. Simply mild the herbs and permit the smoke fill the room.

-Set intentions for safety: Before starting the Ouija board consultation, set clear intentions for safety. You can state your intentions out loud, asking for protection from any horrible entities or energies.

By setting up a shielding barrier, you could create a revel in of protection and protection throughout your Ouija board session. Remember to stay focused on powerful electricity and intentions at a few level in the session, and to shut the consultation nicely at the equal time as you're completed.

By choosing a steady location, you may create a snug and splendid surroundings to your Ouija board session. This can assist reduce distractions and ensure a safe and excellent experience.

Invite effective energies:

Inviting high quality energies is every other essential step to take in advance than the usage of a Ouija board. Here are a few tips on the manner to ask quality energies:

State your purpose to handiest speak with fantastic energies:

Stating your purpose to only communicate with splendid energies is an important step to take in advance than the use of a Ouija board. By placing clean intentions, you could make sure which you are most effective inviting high-quality and loving energies into the consultation.

Here are some guidelines at the manner to state your aim:

-Be unique: Be unique approximately your cause to talk excellent with nice energies. State your purpose really and firmly.

-Use terrific language: Use fantastic language even as pointing out your intention. Avoid the use of poor language, that can entice poor energies. For instance, in area of announcing "I do no longer need to talk with horrific energies", say "I nice want to speak with high-quality and loving energies ».

-Visualize top notch outcomes: Visualize outstanding outcomes for the consultation. Imagine which you are surrounded via way of affection and slight, and that only excellent and loving energies are welcome inside the session.

-Focus on your goal: Focus on your motive in some unspecified time in the future of the session. Keep your intention at the vanguard of your thoughts, and do now not waver from it.

-Trust your instinct: Trust your intuition at the equal time as speakme with the board. If you enjoy that bad energies are present, right now surrender the consultation and cleanse the space.

By declaring your aim to nice talk with splendid energies, you can create a secure and excessive first-rate surroundings on your Ouija board session. This can help promote high-quality communication and decrease the danger of attracting terrible energies.

•Visualize outstanding energy:

Visualizing great energy is a effective approach that permit you to invite awesome energies into your Ouija board session. By visualizing notable power, you can create a excellent and loving surroundings, that might sell remarkable communication and decrease the threat of attracting negative energies.

Here are a few tips on a manner to visualise exquisite strength:

-Close your eyes: Close your eyes and take a few deep breaths. Focus for your breath and permit your body to loosen up.

-Visualize a awesome mild: Visualize a glittery mild surrounding you and your region. Imagine the slight filling the room with love and positivity.

-Focus at the slight: Focus your interest at the moderate and permit it to fill your frame with powerful energy. Imagine the mild flowing via your body, filling each mobile with positivity and love.

-Hold the visualization: Hold the visualization for a couple of minutes, permitting the satisfactory energy to waft through you and your region.

-Repeat effective affirmations: While visualizing the quality strength, repeat immoderate super affirmations to decorate the visualization. For example, you could say "I am surrounded thru way of love and positivity" or "Only effective and loving energies are welcome right here ».

By visualizing fantastic power, you could create a welcoming and high exceptional surroundings in your Ouija board consultation. This can assist promote high high-quality communique and decrease the danger of attracting terrible energies.

Call on spirit courses or angels:

Calling on spirit publications or angels is every other way to invite awesome energy into your Ouija board consultation. Spirit courses and angels are believed to be entities which can be right here to help and protect us. By calling on them, you can ask for his or her steering and safety in the end of the session.

Here are some recommendations on how to call on spirit courses or angels:

-Set your cause: Before calling on spirit guides or angels, set your intention to most effective speak with wonderful energies.

-Close your eyes: Close your eyes and take some deep breaths. Focus on your breath and permit your body to lighten up.

-Ask for protection: Ask your spirit guides or angels to guard you and your region at some stage within the session. You can say something like "I name on my spirit guides and angels to defend me and my vicinity for the duration of this consultation ».

-Ask for guidance: Ask your spirit courses or angels to offer steerage at some point of the session. You can say some component like "I ask my spirit courses and angels to guide me closer to effective and loving verbal exchange in some unspecified time in the future of this consultation ».

-Be open to receiving steering: Be open to receiving guidance from your spirit courses or angels. Trust that they'll be there to help and protect you, and that they'll offer you with the steerage you want.

By calling on spirit guides or angels, you may invite incredible and loving energies into your Ouija board consultation. This can help promote exquisite communication and reduce the threat of attracting horrible energies.

Use first-rate affirmations:

Using great affirmations is every other technique that allows you to let you invite powerful energies into your Ouija board session. Affirmations are extremely good statements that let you shift your mindset and appeal to effective energy.

Here are a few suggestions at the way to apply first rate affirmations:

-Choose fantastic affirmations: Choose outstanding affirmations that resonate with you and your intentions for the session. For example, you may use affirmations consisting of "I am surrounded with the useful resource of love and positivity" or "I best communicate with terrific and loving energies ».

-Repeat affirmations: Repeat your affirmations every silently or out loud before and inside the path of the consultation. This can help make stronger your purpose to most effective communicate with remarkable energies.

-Believe inside the affirmations: Believe in the power of your affirmations. Trust that via repeating powerful affirmations, you're attracting satisfactory power and selling splendid communication.

-Stay targeted: Stay targeted on your affirmations inside the route of the session. This will permit you to stay targeted and tremendous, even if you come upon horrible electricity or reviews.

By using satisfactory affirmations, you could shift your mind-set and lure great energy into your Ouija board session. This can assist sell first rate communique and reduce the threat of attracting horrible energies.

Burn candles or incense:

Burning candles or incense is a not unusual workout a good way to permit you to create a high fine and peaceful ecosystem throughout your Ouija board consultation. Burning candles or incense will let you lighten up and create a chilled environment, which can be conducive to high-quality communication.

Here are some hints at the manner to use candles or incense in the route of your Ouija board session:

- Choose candles or incense: Choose candles or incense that resonate in conjunction with your aim for the session. For instance, you could use lavender-scented candles or incense to promote rest and peace.

- Set up the candles or incense: Set up the candles or incense in a secure place, far from any flammable devices. You can also use candle holders or incense burners to include the flames or ashes.

- Light the candles or incense: Light the candles or incense earlier than you start the session. Take a 2nd to cognizance in your purpose and visualize excellent electricity surrounding you.

- Keep a watch at the candles or incense: Keep a watch constant on the candles or incense within the route of the consultation to make certain they'll be burning adequately. Do not go away the candles or incense unattended.

-Extinguish the candles or incense: Extinguish the candles or incense once you have got were given completed the session. Use a candle snuffer or wet material to extinguish the flames.

By burning candles or incense throughout your Ouija board session, you may create a super and peaceful surroundings that is conducive to excessive high-quality communique. This can assist sell first-rate energy and decrease the hazard of attracting negative energies.

Use crystals:

Using crystals is some other technique that assist you to sell effective power all through your Ouija board consultation. Crystals are believed to have recuperation houses and may be used to increase extremely good energy and defend toward bad energy.

Here are a few tips on the way to use crystals inside the path of your Ouija board session:

-Choose crystals: Choose crystals that resonate together along with your goal for the session. For instance, smooth quartz is a powerful crystal for amplifying immoderate extraordinary electricity, even as amethyst can promote rest and protection.

-Cleanse the crystals: Cleanse the crystals earlier than using them by using way of putting them in salt water or smudging them with sage. This can assist get rid of any terrible electricity that can be related to the crystals.

-Set up the crystals: Set up the crystals across the Ouija board or in a grid formation to create a defensive barrier. You also can keep the crystals on your hand at some diploma inside the session to sell first rate electricity.

-Visualize tremendous energy: Visualize fantastic power surrounding you and the crystals. Focus to your goal and visualize the crystals amplifying excellent electricity and protective you from horrible strength.

-Cleanse the crystals after the session: Cleanse the crystals after the session to get rid of any horrible electricity that may have accumulated at some point of the session.

Using crystals during your Ouija board session can help sell extraordinary electricity and shield closer to terrible energy. By the usage of crystals that resonate along side your purpose for the session, you may boom extremely good power and promote a exquisite and non violent surroundings for communication.

By inviting super energies, you can create a welcoming and safe area in your Ouija board consultation. This can help sell superb conversation and reduce the chance of attracting horrible energies.

Use a defensive talisman:

Using a defensive talisman is each other manner to create a shielding barrier round yourself within the path of a Ouija board consultation. Here are a few pointers for choosing and using a protecting talisman:

Choose a talisman:

Choosing a talisman for protection within the course of a Ouija board session is a non-public desire, as awesome devices may also hold one-of-a-kind meanings and energies for exclusive people. Here are a few common sorts of talismans and their protecting homes:

-Crystals: Certain crystals are believed to have protective homes and can be used as talismans. For instance, black tourmaline is thought to shield in opposition to bad energies and psychic attacks, whilst amethyst is notion to protect in opposition to non secular assaults and psychic vampires.

-Amulets: An amulet is a small item, often worn as earrings, that is believed to have defensive houses. Some not unusual protecting amulets embody the evil eye, the Hamsa, and the Celtic knot.

-Symbols: Certain symbols are believed to have defensive houses, together with the pentagram, it really is typically utilized in Wiccan and Pagan traditions, and the pass, that is normally utilized in Christian traditions.

-Personal objects: A private item, at the facet of a bit of jewelry that holds sentimental fee, can also be used as a talisman. The item want to be cleansed and charged with shielding strength before use.

When deciding on a talisman, it's far critical to pick out one that resonates together along side your personal ideals and intentions. You also can consider the homes of various stones, symbols, and amulets to discover one that aligns along with your desired level of protection. Remember to cleanse and rate your talisman before use, and set clean intentions for it to provide safety in the course of the Ouija board consultation.

- Cleanse the talisman:

Cleansing the talisman is an critical step to make sure that it's far free of any terrible energies or vibrations that might intervene with its protective houses. Here are a few common techniques for cleaning talismans:

-Water: Holding the talisman under on foot water or submerging it in a bowl of salt water is a smooth and effective way to cleanse it. The water need to be jogging or flowing to keep away any horrible energies. After cleansing, make certain to dry the talisman thoroughly.

-Smoke: Burning sage, palo santo, or amazing cleansing herbs and passing the talisman through the smoke can cleanse it of any lousy energies. The smoke should be allowed to clearly surround the talisman.

-Sun or Moonlight: Placing the talisman in direct sunlight or moonlight can recharge and cleanse it. The mild from the sun or moon should be allowed to definitely envelop the talisman.

-Sound: Using a singing bowl, bell, or one-of-a-kind musical tool to create sound vibrations can cleanse the talisman. Simply keep the talisman in one hand and strike the device with the possibility, allowing the sound to clean over the talisman.

Before the use of the talisman for safety throughout a Ouija board session, it's miles critical to cleanse it to cast off any poor energies and vibrations it is able to have picked up. You can pick the approach that resonates with you the most, or try high-quality techniques to find one that works best for you.

Set intentions:

Setting intentions is an vital step to assist reputation your power and direct the outcome of your Ouija board consultation. Here are some tips that will help you set your intentions:

-Be precise: Your intentions have to be specific and easy. Think about what you want to acquire or what you preference to advantage out of your Ouija board session. Maybe you want to connect with a specific loved individual who has exceeded away or are seeking out steerage on a particular hassle. Whatever it's miles, be easy and specific to your aim.

-Use incredible language: Your intentions need to be stated in first-rate language. For example, in region of announcing "I don't want to hear from any poor spirits," say "I first-rate need to speak with first rate energies." This allows to focus your power on what you want to accumulate in area of what you need to avoid.

-Believe for your intentions: It's critical to do not forget on your intentions and trust that they'll come to fruition. Your ideals and energy play a important position within the fulfillment of your Ouija board session, so it's far crucial to approach it with a extraordinary and open thoughts-set.

-Write down your intentions: Writing down your intentions can help to solidify them to your mind and function a reminder in the end of the session. You can hold them close by or possibly location them at the Ouija board itself.

By putting clear and powerful intentions, you could focus your energy and direct the very last consequences of your Ouija board session in the direction of your preferred final results. Remember to approach it with an open and superb thoughts-set and be given as actual with in the device.

Wear or bring the talisman:

Wearing or sporting a talisman in the direction of your Ouija board session is a way to assist guard yourself from horrible energies and to hold superb strength into your region. Here are some hints on the manner to use a talisman:

-Choose a talisman that resonates with you: A talisman can be any item that holds meaning or importance to you, which includes a piece of jewelry, a crystal, or a image. Choose a talisman that you're feeling interested by or that has a completely specific importance for you.

-Cleanse the talisman: Before the use of the talisman, it's far vital to cleanse it of any horrible energy that can be attached to it. You can try this via way of keeping it below walking water, smudging it with sage or palo santo, or leaving it in the slight of the entire moon.

-Charge the talisman: Once the talisman is cleansed, you can charge it along side your intention for the Ouija board consultation. Hold the talisman in your fingers and attention your power on it. Visualize exceptional electricity flowing into the talisman and filling it with moderate.

-Wear or deliver the talisman: During your Ouija board consultation, put on or supply the talisman with you to assist shield your self from terrible energies and to carry wonderful energy into your area. You can also area the talisman at the Ouija board itself or in a super vicinity in the room.

By carrying or sporting a talisman within the direction of your Ouija board session, you could assist to protect yourself from awful energies and bring super electricity into your area. Remember to pick a talisman that resonates with you and to cleanse and price it in advance than the use of it.

Close the consultation well:

Closing the consultation well is an crucial step on the same time as using a Ouija board. It includes well saying good-bye to any spirits or energies which can were communicated with in the direction of the consultation. Failing to gather this could leave the door open for horrible energies or entities to linger.

One way to shut the consultation is to thank the spirits or energies for talking and particular that the session is now completing. You can also ask for any energies or entities that were contacted in some unspecified time in the future of the session to head away and return to their own realm.

Some human beings moreover pick out to cleanse the distance over again after the consultation has ended, using strategies which include burning sage or lighting candles. This can help to similarly remove any residual terrible electricity.

It is vital to keep away from leaving the planchette at the board even as the session is over, as this may moreover leave the door open for terrible strength. Instead, properly shop the board and planchette in a solid region until the following time they will be wanted.

It is likewise advocated to take a damage amongst intervals, in particular if there was any unsettling or awful strength present within the route of the consultation. This permits time to smooth and reset every the physical area and personal electricity.

By the usage of a shielding talisman, you could create a further layer of protection round your self in the course of a Ouija board session. Remember to select a talisman that resonates with you and your intentions, and to set clear intentions for it to provide protection.

Never use the board alone:

Using a Ouija board on my own is normally no longer advocated. It is generally in reality useful to use the board with as a minimum a further individual. This is due to the fact having every different man or woman present can help to offer a experience of grounding and guide all through the session.

When the use of the board by myself, it can be much less complex to grow to be too immersed within the revel in and lose touch with reality. This can reason heightened tension or worry, similarly to prolonged vulnerability to horrible energies or entities.

Having a associate finally of the session can also provide a 2d mindset on any messages or communications acquired thru the board. This can assist to lessen the danger of misinterpretation or false impression, which could occasionally get up at the same time as the usage of the board by myself.

In widespread, it's miles vital to method the use of the Ouija board with appreciate and caution, and to continuously prioritize protection and safety. This consists of having at least a in addition character gift at some stage in the consultation, similarly to following all encouraged precautions and guidelines.

Avoid terrible feelings:

Negative emotions can create a effective power that may lure terrible entities or spirits to the session. These entities can occasionally appear as threatening or adverse, inflicting worry and anxiety in those taking part. Negative feelings can also motive those collaborating inside the session to lose popularity and turn out to be disoriented, foremost to potentially risky results.

To keep away from horrible feelings at some point of a consultation, it's miles essential to take steps to create a excessive outstanding and stable surroundings. This can be finished via using the talisman, putting clean intentions, and calling upon first-rate energies or guides for safety.

Individuals have to ensure that they will be in a peaceful and focused u . S . Before starting the consultation. This may be completed through meditation or rest strategies.

If terrible feelings do arise all through the consultation, it's far important to widely recognized them and release them earlier than persevering with. One manner to do this is thru deep breathing or visualization strategies, specializing in liberating the terrible feelings and bringing in outstanding energies. Participants also can take a brief damage to regroup and ground themselves in advance than continuing.

It is likewise essential to avoid the usage of the Ouija board on the identical time as under the have an effect on of medication or alcohol. These materials can alter notion and judgment, making it tough to stay targeted and right right down to earth within the course of the session. This can increase the chance of bad research and in all likelihood harmful results.

By last calm, focused, and notable at some diploma inside the consultation, contributors can create a safe and green experience whilst the use of a Ouija board.

Don't invite the unknown:

When the use of a Ouija board, it's far important to be careful and aware of the energies you are inviting into your area. One crucial rule to comply with is to avoid inviting the unknown. This approach that you want to not attempt to contact spirits or entities that you recognize not some thing approximately or have by no means encountered earlier than.

Inviting the unknown can be volatile because of the fact you can not expect the person of the energies which could respond on your invitation. There is not any way of understanding if the spirit you're speaking with is benevolent or malevolent, and there may be constantly the chance of attracting terrible energies that could reason harm.

Another reason to keep away from inviting the unknown is that it may attraction to undesirable interest to you and your vicinity. By reaching out to spirits you understand nothing about, you may inadvertently invite one-of-a-kind entities to enroll within the communication. These additional spirits need to have a horrific have an effect on to your consultation and in all likelihood motive damage.

Furthermore, when you invite the unknown, you're starting your self as much as the possibility of encountering entities that might not have your incredible pursuits in mind. They also can furthermore have their private time desk and might use the consultation to govern or mislead you.

When you invite the unknown, you can also lure decrease degree energies which have no longer however developed to a better plane. These entities may be interested by the power of the board but may not have the potential to talk successfully, which could reason confusion and potentially volatile situations.

It is also essential to undergo in thoughts that spirits who're unusual with you can not have your terrific pursuits in thoughts. They won't apprehend how to talk correctly or might not be aware about the damage they is probably inflicting. Therefore, it's miles constantly exceptional to be careful and avoid inviting the unknown.

When the usage of a Ouija board, it's far essential to handiest invite powerful energies that you have a connection with. By preserving off the unknown, you may guard yourself and your region from undesirable energies that could cause damage or manipulate your session. Remember to usually set smooth intentions and use defensive measures to make sure a stable and awesome enjoy.

Set obstacles:

Setting obstacles is vital on the identical time as the use of a Ouija board. It is crucial to have a easy expertise of what shape of communication is appropriate and what is not. It is also important to understand a way to forestall a consultation if matters get out of hand. Setting obstacles permits to maintain control and defend yourself and others from terrible strength and threatening entities.

One way to set barriers is thru determining what shape of questions or subjects are off-limits sooner or later of the consultation. This consists of questions on dying, the future, and private records. It is also vital to determine what form of entities you're inclined to talk with and what kind you aren't. For example, you may want to speak with benevolent spirits but now not with malevolent ones.

Another way to set limitations is through using establishing a easy signal for completing the session. This can be a phrase, a gesture, or a selected movement that indicates the session is over. It is essential to talk this sign to anyone worried within the consultation without a doubt in order that they recognize what to do if topics get uncomfortable or volatile.

It is essential to restrict the quantity of time spent the usage of the Ouija board. Long commands can growth the chance of horrible energy or dangerous entities making touch. It is commonly endorsed to restriction durations to no extra than half of-hour at a time.

Another way to set boundaries is with the beneficial useful resource of the usage of protective devices together with crystals, amulets, or symbols. These may be used to create a protective barrier at some stage in the people and the board. It is important to cleanse and price those devices regularly to ensure their effectiveness.

It is also essential to set obstacles with high-quality people who may be gift in the end of the session. This consists of family individuals, friends, or special people who may be curious or skeptical. It is critical to offer an motive for the dangers concerned inside the use of the Ouija board and to ask for his or her recognize and cooperation during the session.

Finally, it is critical to recall your instincts and set obstacles that enjoy right for you. If at any factor at a few stage within the session you sense uncomfortable or risky, it's miles vital to prevent the consultation without delay. Remember, you are on top of things, and setting obstacles is an essential a part of retaining that manage.

Chapter 7: The Technological Facts In The Back Of The Ouija Board

The Ouija board has been a source of fascination and controversy for many years, with some people believing that it's miles a device for speaking with the spirit global, at the identical time as others dismiss it as a trifling toy. Despite the persevering with debate approximately its validity, the Ouija board has remained a famous and captivating mission for scientists and researchers. In this financial disaster, we're able to find out the scientific theories and studies in the returned of the Ouija board.

While some humans characteristic the board's motion to the spirits, others receive as proper with that it's miles the end result of the ideomotor impact, it truly is a intellectual phenomenon in which an character's subconscious moves have an effect on their bodily actions. The ideomotor impact indicates that the members are unwittingly moving the planchette themselves, in choice to being guided with the resource of any outside strain.

There are research that guide the concept that the Ouija board works because of the ideomotor effect. For example, a have a take a look at executed in the 1970s decided that the board's motion may be attributed to the contributors' subconscious actions. However, there's moreover research that shows that the board's movement can't be described thru the ideomotor impact alone, and that there can be various factors at play.

Another precept regarding the Ouija board's effectiveness is the idea of the "psychic phone idea," which indicates that the board acts as a conduit for the unconscious thoughts to talk with others. This concept proposes that the board's moves aren't the quit result of any supernatural or spiritual pressure, however as an alternative the stop result of the unconscious thoughts's capacity to faucet into time-commemorated recognition and speak thru the board.

Some researchers have proposed that the Ouija board's effectiveness can be associated with quantum physics and the concept of non-locality. This concept shows that the board is capable of get right of entry to records and power from past the physical realm thru quantum entanglement, that's the concept that particles may be related no matter their distance.

The technology in the lower back of the Ouija board is a charming hassle that continues to intrigue scientists and researchers. While a few research help the idea that the board's movement is the quit cease result of the ideomotor impact, others recommend that there can be greater complicated factors at play. In the following sections, we're capable of delve deeper into each of those theories and discover the proof supporting them.

Theories on how the Ouija board works

There are numerous theories approximately how the Ouija board works, and scientists were reading this mysterious device for decades. One of the maximum commonplace theories is the ideomotor impact, which suggests that the movements of the planchette are due to unconscious muscle moves, in desire to any supernatural stress. This method that the individuals within the Ouija board consultation are unknowingly inflicting the planchette to move, often with out figuring out it.

Another idea is that the Ouija board works thru the electricity of perception. This manner that the members are precipitated via way of the expectations and beliefs of others in the business enterprise, that might result in a kind of groupthink or shared attention. The unconscious minds of the members may moreover then create the phantasm of a supernatural pressure guiding the planchette.

Some researchers have moreover cautioned that the Ouija board may additionally furthermore tap into the collective unconscious, a shared pool of facts and reminiscences that exists internal all people. This principle suggests that the planchette moves may be guided via a type of collective intelligence, in choice to any character awareness.

Another concept is that the Ouija board is really a device for having access to the paranormal or religious realm. This concept shows that the board is a conduit for communique with entities from beyond the bodily global, which includes spirits, ghosts, or demons.

Despite the numerous theories about how the Ouija board works, there may be little scientific proof to help any of them. The right nature of the Ouija board remains a mystery, and masses of human beings keep to apply it as a tool for non secular exploration or amusement, at the identical time as others agree with it to be volatile and keep away from it altogether.

Scientific studies on the Ouija board

Scientific research at the Ouija board had been carried out in tries to offer an motive behind its paranormal competencies. One such have a take a look at become finished via neuroscientists, who observed that the movements of the planchette on the Ouija board were the stop stop result of the ideomotor impact. The ideomotor impact is a phenomenon in which the subconscious mind can effect the frame to transport involuntarily, without aware awareness. In the case of the Ouija board, the subconscious thoughts of the individuals may be directing the moves of the planchette, growing the illusion of communique with spirits.

Another have a observe checked out the effects of the Ouija board at the thoughts the usage of electroencephalography (EEG).

The test decided that once individuals used the Ouija board, there was extended interest within the regions of the brain associated with self-referential thinking and semantic processing. This suggests that the usage of the Ouija board may be a shape of self-delivered on hypnosis, with the contributors' subconscious minds guiding the actions of the planchette.

Despite these clinical reasons, there are although a few unexplained phenomena related to the Ouija board. For example, there are opinions of the board spelling out messages which can be highly unique and correct, which some consider can not be defined via the ideomotor effect by myself.

Additionally, there are numerous anecdotal bills of the board shifting with none apparent physical contact, this is tough to give an explanation for using traditional scientific theories.

It's properly nicely well worth noting that some researchers have criticized the methodologies of those studies, arguing that they do now not definitely account for the complexities of the Ouija board enjoy. Furthermore, some trust that the Ouija board may tap proper proper right into a realm of recognition beyond the bodily global, making it tough to absolutely supply an explanation for using traditional clinical techniques.

While clinical research have shed a few moderate on the workings of the Ouija board, there can be despite the fact that lots that stays mysterious and unexplained. Whether or no longer the board in reality lets in communique with spirits or is without a doubt the end result of subconscious movements, it remains a charming and regularly arguable device for those interested in the magical.

Skeptical viewpoints on the Ouija board

Skeptical viewpoints at the Ouija board advise that the movement of the planchette is because of the ideomotor impact. This effect occurs while a person's unconscious movements are guided thru their mind or beliefs, with out their conscious cognizance. In the case of the Ouija board, skeptics argue that the moves of the planchette are inspired with the resource of the contributors' unconscious mind and ideals, in preference to any outside supernatural forces.

Skeptics additionally point out that the accuracy of the statistics provided with the aid of the Ouija board can be attributed to a phenomenon called the "Barnum impact," that is the tendency for people to trust commonplace statements approximately themselves as being correct and mainly tailored to them, even supposing they may be now not. This way that the indistinct and fashionable messages acquired via the Ouija board may additionally additionally appear in my opinion significant to the participants, even if they may be no longer truely accurate or coming from a supernatural supply.

Skeptics argue that the meant supernatural powers of the Ouija board have by no means been scientifically tested, and that the reports human beings have with the board can be defined through herbal, intellectual, and social elements.

They suggest that the Ouija board may be visible as a form of leisure or a tool for exploring one's private unconscious, in location of a way of speakme with spirits or amazing supernatural entities.

Despite the skepticism surrounding the Ouija board, some researchers have attempted to study its results in a systematic context. For example, a have a look at posted in the Journal of Nervous and Mental Disease in 2012 examined the results of the Ouija board on people' tension tiers and decided that it had no good sized effect on anxiety. Another have a look at posted inside the identical journal in 2014 determined that folks who believed in the paranormal have been much more likely to characteristic which means to the actions of the planchette than folks who did not.

In stop, whilst the medical evidence for the supernatural powers of the Ouija board is missing, the board keeps to fascinate and intrigue human beings round the world. Skeptics argue that the movements of the planchette are because of herbal mental and social elements, while believers maintain that the board can talk with the spirit international. Regardless of one's attitude, the Ouija board remains a completely unique cultural artifact with a rich history and ongoing controversy.

Chapter 8: Real-Existence Research With The Ouija Board

The Ouija board has been a popular tool for talking with the spiritual realm for over a century, and as such, there were many reminiscences and reviews associated with its use. Some humans have had great research that have helped them connect to loved ones who've handed on, at the same time as others have had terrible stories that have left them feeling scared and traumatized. In this financial disaster, we will discover a number of those real-life reviews, every excellent and awful, and try to understand what can also have delivered approximately them.

True memories of humans's tales with the Ouija board

Many humans who have used the Ouija board file feeling an excessive and palpable strength at some stage in their classes. Some describe feeling a chilly breeze or seeing devices circulate across the room.

Others declare to have visible apparitions or skilled unexplainable phenomena.

One common trouble amongst many Ouija board customers is the enjoy of receiving messages from deceased loved ones. People file feeling a robust connection to their departed own family contributors or buddies and receiving messages that they experience could not have come from in fact every person else.

Some customers have said feeling a robust presence or power that they believe to be demonic or poor in nature. These opinions may be very horrifying and can go away lasting intellectual outcomes on the man or woman.

Other customers have said feeling a revel in of peace or enlightenment in the direction of their Ouija board classes. They describe feeling a connection to a better electricity or religious strength that permits them to better apprehend their area within the global.

In a few instances, human beings have recommended experiencing bodily signs and symptoms and signs at some point of or after the usage of the Ouija board. These signs and signs and symptoms can range from mild headaches or nausea to more severe issues like seizures or fainting spells.

There were opinions of human beings turning into obsessed with using the Ouija board and spending endless hours speakme with spirits. Some have even claimed that the board has turn out to be an addiction for them, inflicting them to forget about about specific elements of their lives.

While many humans take delivery of as actual with that the Ouija board can be a device for speaking with spirits, others view it as a simplest psychological phenomenon. These skeptics argue that the moves of the planchette are due to the customers' unconscious movements and that any messages obtained are really a contemplated image of the users' very own mind and goals.

Some humans agree with that the Ouija board may be a volatile device that should now not be used without right training or steerage. They argue that the board may be utilized by malevolent spirits to gain get right of entry to to the bodily international and motive damage to the customers.

There had been numerous money owed of human beings experiencing lousy outcomes after using the Ouija board, inclusive of bodily damage, emotional distress, or maybe ownership. These opinions have led some to accept as true with that the board is a gateway to the spirit worldwide that ought to not be opened gently.

Despite the talk surrounding the Ouija board, it remains a popular tool for the ones seeking out to speak with spirits. Many people trust that the board can provide a totally particular and powerful revel in, permitting them to connect to loved ones who have handed on or gain a deeper information of the religious realm.

As with any tool or exercise, it's far critical to technique the Ouija board with caution and recognize. Users need to be privy to the potential risks and take steps to guard themselves from terrible electricity or unwanted spirits.

Whether you acquire as right with within the spiritual power of the Ouija board or no longer, it's far easy that the device has had a profound effect on limitless humans's lives. Its capability to connect human beings with the unseen world has involved and intrigued human beings for generations, and its legacy is excellent to hold for decades to return.

The risks of the use of the Ouija board

there are numerous functionality risks associated with the use of the Ouija board, each bodily and intellectual. Some of the physical risks encompass by hazard burning oneself with candles or incense, or maybe tripping and falling in the darkish if proper lighting isn't always used. However, the extra immoderate risks are frequently psychological or religious in nature.

One of the precept risks of the use of the Ouija board is that it may appeal to horrible or malevolent entities. Some human beings endure in mind that the ones entities are drawn to the board itself, at the same time as others endure in thoughts that they will be interested in the strength this is generated at some stage in a session. Regardless of the cause, it's miles critical to recall that now not all spirits are benevolent and a few can also have unwell intentions toward the ones the use of the board.

Another chance is the potential for the board to grow to be a gateway or portal for horrific entities to enter into our international. Some humans believe that the usage of the Ouija board can open up a doorway some of the physical realm and the spiritual realm, and that this doorway can allow entities to bypass over. This can be particularly unstable if the entity that comes via is malevolent or dangerous in a few way.

Furthermore, the Ouija board additionally can be a supply of mental damage. It is not unusual for people to turn out to be captivated with the board and the messages that it produces. This can result in an terrible preoccupation with the board and the spirit international, which can purpose anxiety, depression, and particular mental troubles.

Using the Ouija board can from time to time bring about the development of psychic abilities, which can be every a present and a curse. While some people can also find out those skills to be empowering and beneficial, others also can find out them overwhelming or perhaps horrifying.

Using the Ouija board also can bring about a loss of private strength and control. Some people report feeling as despite the fact that they will be being controlled or manipulated thru the spirits they're speakme with, and this loss of manage can be very unsettling.

Another chance of using the Ouija board is that it may attraction to the eye of terrible entities which can join themselves to the consumer. These entities can motive quite quite a number bodily, emotional, and intellectual signs and signs, collectively with depression, anxiety, fatigue, or maybe physical infection.

Using the Ouija board may be addictive, and a few humans may moreover moreover discover it tough to prevent using it after they have started out out. This dependancy may be fueled thru the experience of power and connection that comes from communicating with spirits, however it may also be fueled via a preference for validation or interest.

Furthermore, the use of the Ouija board can also result in the manipulation or deception of the users. Some entities can also additionally furthermore fake to be a person or a few detail they'll be now not, and this will bring about confusion, frustration, or even harm.

Another hazard of using the Ouija board is that it could reason rifts in relationships, mainly if one man or woman worried within the consultation is extra skeptical or uncomfortable with the tool than the others. This can bring about feelings of mistrust, resentment, or maybe outright warfare.

While the Ouija board may be a charming and interesting tool for exploring the spirit global, it's far important to method it with caution and recognize. The capability dangers related to its use are very real, and it is important to be aware of them in advance than searching to speak with the unknown. By taking suitable precautions and using the board responsibly, however, it is possible to have a steady and quality experience with this enigmatic tool.

The ability outcomes of using the Ouija board

While using the Ouija board may be interesting or perhaps thrilling to a few, it's miles crucial to be privy to the functionality effects and risks worried. Here are some capability consequences which could result from the use of the Ouija board:

Inviting poor energies:

Inviting horrible energies is one of the maximum extremely good dangers of the usage of the Ouija board. When the usage of the board, you are setting up up a portal to the spirit worldwide, and you in no way understand what form of energy may also moreover come through. Negative energies can attach themselves to individuals or observe them home, inflicting misery, infection, and even ownership. These energies may be unstable and difficult to eliminate with out professional help.

Another capability outcome of inviting negative energies is the manifestation of bad activities in a unmarried's existence. When people intentionally or via twist of fate invite horrible power, it is able to have a ripple impact on their lives. They may also moreover revel in a sequence of unfortunate sports, in conjunction with accidents, illnesses, and economic troubles. Negative energies also can result in a lower in intellectual and emotional fitness, collectively with despair, tension, and paranoia.

Another threat of the usage of the Ouija board is the capacity for deception. Negative energies might also cover themselves as brilliant spirits or loved ones, predominant humans to keep in mind they're receiving steerage or messages from a relied on source. However, those energies also can have ulterior motives and use deception to benefit manage over an person's thoughts, feelings, and actions.

The Ouija board can lure and growth lousy energy already found in a place. If the board is utilized in a place with a information of horrible occasions or emotions, it could intensify those energies and cause them to more hard to dispel.

One capability cease result of the use of the Ouija board is the mental effect it is able to have on people. It can result in a lack of sense of manage, as human beings can also sense that they may be not on top of things of their thoughts or movements. Additionally, it may motive feelings of guilt, shame, and tension, as humans may additionally experience that they've opened themselves as a lot as terrible power and located themselves in hazard.

Another capability danger of the usage of the Ouija board is the possibility of creating bad thought forms or entities. These are created by means of way of poor electricity and can linger prolonged after the board has been positioned away. Negative concept office work can result in disturbances within the surroundings and the creation of horrible electricity that could have an effect on human beings inside the surrounding vicinity.

Using the Ouija board can cause an addiction to the board and the act of speakme with the spirit international. This dependancy can be dangerous, crucial to a loss of control over one's life and an obsession with the board. It can reason bad affects on highbrow, bodily, and emotional fitness and disrupt relationships and each day lifestyles.

Using the Ouija board can be a dangerous and probable unstable interest. It is vital to be aware about the potential consequences and dangers earlier than using the board and to take precautions to protect oneself and others.

Psychic assaults:

Psychic attacks are some other capability risk of using the Ouija board. Psychic attacks are times wherein a person or entity intentionally goals and harms each other man or woman the use of their private power or psychic skills. When the use of the Ouija board, individuals can also unknowingly invite horrible or malevolent entities to talk with them. These entities may also additionally attempt to control the client or even attack them psychically.

Psychic assaults may additionally have a big fashion of effects on the sufferer, which encompass bodily and emotional signs and symptoms. Some not unusual bodily signs and signs and symptoms of a psychic attack embody complications, fatigue, and frame aches. Emotional signs and signs might also moreover moreover encompass anxiety, depression, and feelings of paranoia. In severe times, a psychic attack also can even cause possession via the usage of a horrific entity.

It is critical to be aware that not certainly every body believes in psychic attacks, and some skeptics also can brush aside them as surely highbrow phenomena. However, those who've expert such assaults can also moreover attest to their reality and the capacity risks of using the Ouija board.

To defend oneself from psychic assaults at the same time as the usage of the Ouija board, it is vital to set sturdy intentions and limitations before beginning the consultation. It is likewise encouraged to name on protecting energies or entities, which encompass angels or spirit publications, to help in keeping the session strong. Additionally, wearing or carrying a shielding talisman, which consist of a crystal or piece of jewellery, can also offer brought protection.

The potential for psychic assaults on the equal time as the usage of the Ouija board highlights the significance of coming close to its use with caution and apprehend. It is critical to generally prioritize private protection and properly-being on the same time as conducting any non secular or paranormal practices.

Attachment of terrible entities:

Another potential danger of the use of the Ouija board is the attachment of horrible entities. When you open your self as much as communication with the spirit worldwide, you can inadvertently entice lousy energies which can join themselves to you or the gap in which you are the use of the board. These entities may be indignant, malicious, or seeking out to reason damage, and they may not go away without trouble.

Once an entity has related itself, it may purpose some of terrible results, on the side of physical infection, emotional misery, and intellectual issues. Some humans have stated experiencing sudden modifications in conduct or man or woman, together with becoming aggressive or withdrawn. Others have mentioned feeling continuously uninterested in energy or experiencing unexplained mood swings.

Removing a awful entity can be a tough and prolonged way, often requiring the help of a expert which embody a psychic, shaman, or electricity healer. It is critical to take precautions to avoid attracting terrible energies in the first place and to are looking for assist if you suspect which you or a person else has been affected.

It is also crucial to word that the attachment of bad entities isn't always confined to the usage of the Ouija board. Any sort of non secular communique or interaction with the spirit international consists of a capability chance of attracting poor energies. However, the Ouija board is regularly seen as a specifically unstable tool because it allows for direct and unfiltered communique with spirits, without the safety of a educated practitioner or medium.

It is crucial to be aware about the potential dangers of using the Ouija board and to approach it with caution and recognize. If you select out to apply the board, it's miles advocated that you do so with a clean intention, a sturdy revel in of protection, and inside the presence of a professional practitioner or medium. If you revel in any awful effects, are seeking out help right now.

False or deceptive records:

Another risk of the use of the Ouija board is the opportunity of receiving fake or misleading information. Since the board works via the participants' unconscious minds, it is viable for them to accumulate messages that aren't correct or reliable. The messages will also be recommended via way of the people' expectations, beliefs, and biases, that would further distort the accuracy of the statistics received.

In some instances, the individuals can also deliberately control the board to gain faux or deceptive records. This may be carried out for diverse reasons, together with to prank others, to expose a issue, or to advantage interest. However, such actions will have intense outcomes, because of the fact the recipients of the fake facts can also act upon it and make alternatives based totally definitely totally on it.

Furthermore, it's far crucial to be conscious that the Ouija board isn't always a dependable device for divination or spiritual steering. Its accuracy and effectiveness have no longer been scientifically proven, and it ought to now not be used instead for professional recommendation or treatment. Relying too carefully on the board for critical selections or existence choices can motive awful outcomes and remorse.

The Ouija board may be a unstable device that want to be approached with caution and appreciate. The capability results of the usage of the board encompass inviting terrible energies, psychic assaults, attachment of horrific entities, and receiving fake or deceptive records. It's vital to be aware of those dangers and to take measures to shield oneself in advance than and after the use of the board. Ultimately, the great course of movement may be to keep away from the use of the Ouija board altogether and to are attempting to find steering and advice from greater reliable resources.

Increased susceptibility to terrible affects:

Another ability risk of the use of the Ouija board is the prolonged susceptibility to bad affects. When people have interaction in Ouija board periods, they will grow to be greater open to terrible energies and affects. This can bring about a number of horrible effects, along aspect increased tension, despair, and mood swings.

The use of the Ouija board can also result in an increase in addictive behavior, as individuals may additionally additionally end up hooked on the sensation of electricity or manage that comes from using the board. This addiction can then bring about an elevated vulnerability to terrible affects and behaviors.

The Ouija board also can serve as a gateway to terrific terrible or dangerous spiritual practices, which encompass black magic or unique kinds of witchcraft. This can lead human beings down a dangerous and possibly unfavourable path, causing them to engage in risky or illegal sports sports.

There is likewise the capability for highbrow harm while using the Ouija board. For example, people may enjoy confusion, disorientation, or perhaps psychosis due to the usage of the board. This can be especially dangerous for people with pre-present highbrow health conditions, as it may exacerbate their symptoms and cause similarly misery.

Using the Ouija board also can reason religious and emotional turmoil. Individuals can also enjoy emotions of guilt, shame, or fear due to using the board, particularly if they take delivery of as real with they've contacted terrible entities or spirits. This can bring about emotions of isolation or alienation, as humans may also additionally revel in that they can't confide in others about their reports.

The risks of using the Ouija board ought to now not be taken lightly. While a few humans may also have awesome testimonies the usage of the board, the functionality for terrible outcomes is massive. As such, it is vital to carefully don't forget the functionality risks earlier than figuring out to use the board, and to take suitable precautions to make certain which you are blanketed from damage.

Interference with non-public beliefs or religious practices:

Another capability threat of the usage of the Ouija board is the interference it may have with personal ideals or religious practices. Some people can also moreover feel that the use of the board goes in competition to their non secular ideals or personal values. For example, some spiritual corporations agree with that the Ouija board is a tool of the satan or is used to communicate with malevolent spirits.

Using the board may additionally warfare with personal ideals about demise and the afterlife. The idea of speakme with the vain via a board may be unsettling or perhaps offensive to three human beings. Additionally, the board's messages may also warfare with the man or woman's beliefs approximately the person of the afterlife, causing confusion or distress.

The Ouija board can doubtlessly motive a loss of faith in one's private ideals or non secular practices. If an individual gets messages through the board that contradict their beliefs or research, they may begin to question their faith and conflict with doubt and uncertainty.

It is important to word that the potential interference with private ideals or religious practices is not confined to folks who actively use the Ouija board. Simply being uncovered to the board and its messages via media or social circles also can have an effect on an character's beliefs and values.

The potential interference with personal ideals or spiritual practices highlights the importance of thinking about one's values and beliefs earlier than attractive with the Ouija board. It is critical to approach the board with an open mind, but additionally to preserve a strong revel in of self and private values.

Difficulty disconnecting:

Another capability hazard of the use of the Ouija board is the hassle in disconnecting from the session. Even if the participants close to the session properly, there may be a risk that they may however feel a lingering presence or strength spherical them. This can result in feelings of anxiety, unease, or maybe paranoia. In a few instances, humans have suggested experiencing nightmares, hallucinations, and specific disturbing phenomena prolonged after the usage of the Ouija board.

Some humans also can end up hooked on using the Ouija board, searching out an increasing number of periods in an try to connect to the alternative element. This can purpose a risky obsession with the magical, and may interfere with their capability to characteristic in every day lifestyles. Some human beings also can even begin to forget approximately their obligations and relationships as a manner to preserve the usage of the board.

Another ability end result of the use of the Ouija board is that it could reason rifts in relationships most of the people.

This can arise if one character becomes glad that the board is offering accurate statistics, whilst each other man or woman remains skeptical. Disagreements can upward push up over whether or not or no longer the information provided with the useful resource of the board is actual or imagined, and this will create tension and mistrust among pals or own family participants.

It is vital to phrase that many religious and cultural traditions consider the usage of the Ouija board to be taboo or perhaps sinful.

For example, some Christians take delivery of as real with that the board is a device of the devil and that the usage of it can invite demonic have an effect on into one's life. Similarly, many Indigenous cultures take into account that speakme with the vain in this way is disrespectful and may anger the spirits. If a person's personal ideals or practices are in war with the use of the Ouija board, they may experience feelings of guilt or disgrace after the usage of it.

While the Ouija board may be a charming and charming device for talking with the magical, it is crucial to be aware of the functionality risks and outcomes of the use of it. These can embody inviting horrible energies, psychic attacks, attachment of terrible entities, faux or deceptive information, extended susceptibility to bad affects, interference with personal beliefs or non secular practices, trouble disconnecting, or perhaps rifts in relationships. Before identifying to use the board, it's miles critical to remember those risks and to continue with warning.

Increased worry or tension:

When human beings use the Ouija board, they're starting themselves up to the unknown and the magical. This can cause worry and tension, in particular if the enjoy is terrible. Many human beings document feeling a revel in of unease or pain all through and after the usage of the board, and those emotions can linger for a long term.

Using the Ouija board might also even motive or worsen tension problems, together with panic attacks or generalized anxiety disease. This is because of the reality the experience of speakme with spirits or entities beyond our bodily truth may be overwhelming and unsettling for some humans.

The fear and tension associated with the Ouija board can spill over into one in every of a type regions of someone's lifestyles. For example, they will end up extra stressful or paranoid in popular, or they may grow to be greater worrying about demise and the afterlife.

It is important to phrase that those functionality outcomes are not skilled by way of everyone who makes use of the Ouija board. However, it's miles vital to be privy to the risks and to technique the board with warning and understand. It is likewise essential to take note of your instincts and save you using the board in case you revel in uncomfortable or risky in any way.

In order to restriction the threat of elevated fear or anxiety, it is essential to set obstacles and to take breaks amongst instructions. It is likewise beneficial to have a guide gadget of friends or loved ones who can offer consolation and reassurance.

While the Ouija board can be a charming device for exploring the paranormal, it is not without its dangers.

Increased fear or tension is one capability impact of the usage of the board, and it's far vital to approach the revel in with warning and appreciate. By putting obstacles, taking breaks, and searching out assist, people can decrease the hazard of terrible outcomes and characteristic a more awesome experience with the board.

Physical damage:

While it's far unusual, there had been reviews of physical harm because of using the Ouija board. Some humans have cautioned feeling physically worn-out or experiencing unexplained bruises or scratches after the usage of the board. There have moreover been instances in which people have claimed to were driven or attacked with the aid of manner of unseen forces at the same time as the use of the board.

One capability motive of this bodily harm is the concept of psychokinetic electricity. This is the principle that the human thoughts has the capability to steer physical devices and sports through the energy of idea. It is possible that the extreme attention and emotional electricity this is frequently worried in the usage of the Ouija board need to result in the accidental launch of psychokinetic power, that can occur in physical strategies.

Another possibility is that horrible entities or spirits may be inquisitive about the electricity this is created at some point of Ouija board classes, and might are attempting to find to damage or very own individuals who are the use of the board. While that is a arguable concept, many human beings who have had bad research with the Ouija board believe that they have been targeted via malevolent entities.

It is vital to be aware that the capability for physical damage isn't always the handiest hazard associated with the Ouija board, and it is not the maximum commonplace. However, it's far vital to be aware about this danger and to method the usage of the board with warning and understand.

Addiction or obsession:

Another capacity risk of the use of the Ouija board is the chance of dependancy or obsession. For some people, the enjoy of using the Ouija board can be exciting and exhilarating, main them to emerge as hooked on the exercising. This dependancy can motive an obsession with communicating with the spirits and might in the long run devour the man or woman's lifestyles.

Those who emerge as hooked on the usage of the Ouija board also can discover that they cannot function generally with out it. They can also spend all their loose time the usage of the board or seeking out new opportunities to speak with spirits. This can result in neglecting critical obligations, together with artwork, faculty, and relationships.

Addiction to the usage of the Ouija board can also motive monetary stress, as people may additionally moreover spend money on steeply-priced Ouija board devices or psychic readings to decorate their experience. In some cases, people may furthermore are searching for out the offerings of a expert medium or psychic, which can be highly-priced.

Addiction to the usage of the Ouija board also can have poor effects on intellectual fitness. The consistent pursuit of communique with spirits can bring about heightened stages of anxiety, strain, and paranoia. This can ultimately reason intellectual health problems which includes depression and tension problems.

It is critical to word that addiction or obsession with the Ouija board isn't always not unusual and typically only takes location in a small minority of people. However, it is despite the fact that a functionality chance that ought to no longer be unnoticed.

While the usage of the Ouija board also can seem innocent and a laugh, it may furthermore include an entire lot of capability risks and risks. It is crucial to approach the exercise with warning and apprehend, and to be aware of the capability results that could upward push up.

Strain on relationships:

Using the Ouija board also can cause a strain on relationships. People who grow to be obsessed on using the board can also forget about their private and expert duties, inflicting conflicts with own family individuals, buddies, and buddies. Loved ones may additionally additionally

additionally become involved about the individual's conduct and nicely-being, which could motive tension and pressure on the connection. Additionally, if one individual in a courting is uncomfortable with the concept of the use of the Ouija board and the other is insistent on the use of it, this may create tension and war.

If a terrible entity is thought to have associated itself to a person who has used the Ouija board, this will create tension and pressure on relationships. The individual also can begin to showcase erratic or unfavorable conduct, which can be scary for those spherical them. This can purpose the breakdown of relationships and social isolation for the character experiencing the negative outcomes of the Ouija board.

In some instances, using the Ouija board can also additionally reason the development of new relationships, along with with spirits or entities believed to be contacted thru the board. These relationships can turn out to be obsessive, with people spending growing quantities of time speakme with those entities to the detriment in their private relationships.

It's moreover possible for the usage of the Ouija board to create tension and conflict internal spiritual organizations. Some spiritual corporations view the board as a device for speaking with demons or other horrible entities, and the usage of it may be seen as a contravention of non secular beliefs or practices. This can result in struggle with others within the religious community, inflicting pressure on those relationships.

The use of the Ouija board can cause distrust or maybe betrayal inside relationships. People may also additionally feel deceived or betrayed by using others who have happy them to use the board or who have misled them approximately its ability results. This can create emotions of anger, resentment, and distrust that can be hard to overcome.

Negative have an effect on on intellectual health:

One of the maximum large dangers of using the Ouija board is the functionality negative impact it can have on one's intellectual health. Many people who use the board report experiencing excessive fear, anxiety, or even paranoia at some point of and after their lessons. This may be especially real for folks which might be already suffering with highbrow fitness troubles which includes melancholy or tension.

Some folks that use the Ouija board also can end up captivated with it, essential to a compulsion to use it often. This can interfere with their each day lives and motive big distress. In some instances, this obsession can motive addiction, which can be hard to overcome.

The Ouija board can also moreover cause an increased hazard of growing intellectual health troubles which include dissociative identification illness (DID) or psychosis. These conditions contain a detachment from truth and may be prompted or exacerbated thru reminiscences collectively with the usage of the board. It is critical to be aware that while the ones situations are fairly uncommon, they may be excessive and may have a good sized effect on one's lifestyles.

Furthermore, the use of the Ouija board can also motive sleep disturbances, together with nightmares and insomnia. The excessive emotions and thoughts that may upward thrust up ultimately of a session can carry over into sleep and effect the remarkable of rest one gets. Over time, this will cause chronic sleep deprivation, which can make contributions to pretty a range of physical and highbrow fitness issues.

The Ouija board's capability lousy have an impact on on intellectual fitness can strain relationships with cherished ones. Friends and own family individuals might not recognize the enchantment of the use of the board and can be concerned approximately the impact it is having at the individual's properly-being. This can bring about war and tension, which may be difficult to navigate and treatment.

While using the Ouija board can also moreover seem like harmless a laugh, it's miles vital to bear in mind the ability consequences carefully. The lousy impact it is able to have on one's intellectual fitness isn't to be taken lightly, and customers want to technique the board with warning and recognize. If one is suffering with intellectual fitness troubles, it's far advocated to keep away from the use of the board altogether.

Chapter 9: The Spiritual And Religious Components Of The Ouija Board

The Ouija board has been a subject of hobby and problem for diverse non secular corporations and spiritual ideals, with some viewing it as a tool of verbal exchange with the spirit international and others condemning it as a tool of the devil. The board's capacity to speak with the unknown has been a supply of fascination for individuals who trust within the life of spirits and the afterlife, as well as parents which may be curious approximately the unknown. This monetary spoil explores the various spiritual and non secular ideals surrounding the Ouija board and how they've original perceptions of its use.

Different cultural beliefs and practices surrounding the Ouija board

The Ouija board has been a part of non secular and non secular practices for the duration of numerous cultures and notion systems for centuries. Different cultural beliefs and practices surrounding the Ouija board often range notably, with a few viewing it as a innocent tool for communique with spirits and others viewing it as a tool for demonic ownership and religious harm.

In a few African cultures, the Ouija board is viewed as a effective device for speakme with ancestors and spirits. In Haiti, as an example, the Ouija board is regularly used in Voodoo ceremonies as a manner of contacting the useless. Similarly, in effective Native American cultures, the Ouija board is used for divination and communication with spirits.

In a few Eastern cultures, the Ouija board is regarded as a device for spiritual growth and self-discovery. In Japan, as an example, the Ouija board is regularly used as a shape of meditation and self-reflected photo. In China, the Ouija board is utilized in Taoist practices as a way of communicating with spirits and gaining spiritual insights.

In Western manner of life, the Ouija board has been related to each spiritualism and occult practices. In the late nineteenth and early 20th centuries, the Ouija board was popularized as a tool for communicating with the lifeless within the route of the Spiritualist motion. However, with the rise of the occult and New Age movements, the Ouija board has come to be related to darker religious practices and the capability for demonic ownership.

Some Christian organizations view the Ouija board as a tool of the satan and actively discourage its use. Other spiritual agencies, which includes Wiccans and Pagans, can also use the Ouija board as a part of their spiritual practices.

Despite the variations in cultural ideals and practices surrounding the Ouija board, one common thread is the notion that it's far a effective tool for talking with spirits and the supernatural realm. Whether considered as a innocent shape of divination or a device for demonic ownership, the Ouija board keeps to maintain an area in non secular and spiritual practices across the world.

The Ouija board's connection to the supernatural and the paranormal

The Ouija board is frequently related to the supernatural and paranormal due to its intended functionality to speak with entities past the physical realm. Some humans trust that the board is a portal to the spirit world and that it permits spirits or certainly one of a kind entities to speak with the residing. This connection to the supernatural and paranormal has been a subject of interest for hundreds people, at the side of paranormal investigators, spiritualists, and those interested by the occult.

Many cultures spherical the arena have their own beliefs about the afterlife and the existence of spirits. In some cultures, the belief in spirits is deeply ingrained in each day life, and using tool similar to the Ouija board is seen as a manner to hook up with the spirit global. However, unique cultures view the Ouija board with suspicion and even worry, as it's far seen as a device which could enchantment to malevolent spirits or demons.

Some human beings who have used the Ouija board have stated experiencing supernatural or paranormal phenomena, which incorporates devices transferring on their personal, atypical sounds or voices, or maybe sightings of apparitions or ghosts. These stories have led some to accept as true with that the board is actually capable of speakme with the other thing. However, others continue to be skeptical and feature the ones stories to mental or herbal causes.

The connection most of the Ouija board and the supernatural has moreover been explored in popular manner of existence, collectively with films, tv indicates, and books. The board has been featured in horror films and remarkable works of fiction that explore the paranormal or supernatural, often portraying it as a tool that may unleash darkish and dangerous forces.

Despite its affiliation with the supernatural and paranormal, the Ouija board stays a controversial and regularly misunderstood device. While some accept as real with that it can provide a real connection to the spirit international, others view it as a trifling activity or hoax. The debate keeps amongst believers and skeptics alike, without a clean consensus at the real nature of the board's connection to the supernatural.

Religious evaluations and criticisms of the Ouija board

Religious critiques and criticisms of the Ouija board range extensively all through one-of-a-type faiths and denominations. Many religions view the use of Ouija forums as unstable and forbidden, while others be given as real with it to be a device for speaking with the useless or one in every of a type entities. Here are a few examples of diverse spiritual views at the Ouija board:

Christianity:

In Christianity, using the Ouija board is normally discouraged, if now not outright condemned, because of its connection to the occult and capability for awful spiritual affect. Many Christians accept as true with that the board is a device of Satan or exceptional malevolent entities, and that using it opens the consumer as lots as demonic possession or oppression.

Some Christian organizations circulate as some distance as to mention that the Ouija board is a shape of divination, it truly is explicitly prohibited within the Bible. The e book of Deuteronomy, as an example, warns towards attempting to find knowledge from the useless or one of a kind non secular resources outside of God, pointing out that such practices are an abomination.

Moreover, a few Christian government declare that the Ouija board may additionally have a dangerous impact on the soul, major humans down a route of religious destruction. It is likewise said to transport in competition to the crucial principle of religion, which requires human beings to recollect in God's plan for their lives in preference to trying to find steerage from other resources.

However, no longer all Christians proportion this view, and there are various who agree with that the Ouija board is honestly a harmless recreation or tool for conversation with spirits. Some even argue that it can be used for particular, together with within the case of looking for steering from deceased loved ones or assisting to resolve mysteries.

Regardless of man or woman ideals, it's far crucial to be aware that using the Ouija board is a non-public choice and need to be approached with warning and recognize for one's non-public religious beliefs and practices.

Islam:

In Islam, the usage of the Ouija board is considered haram or forbidden as it's miles believed to be a shape of divination and looking for knowledge of the unseen, that's precisely prohibited.

Islam furthermore teaches that verbal exchange with the dead isn't always possible, and any try to perform that is considered an act of disbelief. Therefore, the usage of the Ouija board to speak with spirits or deceased loved ones is considered as a violation of Islamic beliefs.

In a few Muslim global locations, the possession and sale of the Ouija board is unlawful, and those caught using it can face punishment. Some Islamic pupils warn toward the risks of the use of the Ouija board, stating that it could result in possession thru evil spirits, intellectual problems, or perhaps dying.

Some Muslims may also moreover nevertheless use the Ouija board, specially people who aren't strictly adherent to Islamic teachings. In those times, it's miles frequently seemed as a form of entertainment in choice to a essential spiritual practice.

The Islamic stance on the Ouija board is taken into consideration taken into consideration one in all sturdy condemnation and prohibition, with a perception that it is going toward the essential teachings of the faith.

Judaism:

In Judaism, the use of the Ouija board is normally discouraged, if no longer outright prohibited, as it is taken into consideration to be a form of divination, it honestly is taken into consideration as a violation of the

Jewish prohibition in opposition to consulting with mediums or necromancers (Deuteronomy 18:10-12). According to Jewish notion, pleasant God has the power to speak with the useless, and attempting to attain this via the Ouija board or distinct way is visible as a task to God's authority.

In Jewish tradition, the vain are not to be disturbed or communicated with, as doing so can bring about bad consequences. The exercising of talking with the dead is taken into consideration as risky and probably beginning oneself up to malevolent non secular forces. Additionally, using the Ouija board may be visible as a form of idolatry, as it entails seeking out steerage or statistics from belongings other than God.

While there can be some Jewish individuals or groups who do use the Ouija board, it is usually not standard in the large Jewish network. Rabbis and considered one of a type non secular leaders may additionally strongly discourage or limit its use, mainly among more youthful those who may be greater prone to its allure.

In summary, within the Jewish religion, the use of the Ouija board is normally discouraged or prohibited due to its affiliation with divination, this is considered a violation of Jewish law, as well as its ability to disturb the vain and open oneself as masses as bad spiritual forces.

Hinduism:

Hinduism is a severa faith with many one-of-a-type ideals and practices, and as such, there is no single unified view at the Ouija board. However, a few Hindus do not forget that using the Ouija board may be a volatile workout which could entice lousy energies and entities. They believe that these horrible energies and entities can motive damage to folks who use the board and can also purpose disruptions to their non secular practices.

Others view the Ouija board as a device that may be used to connect with non secular energies and entities in a exquisite and high quality way. They receive as real with that the board may be used to speak with loved ones who've passed on or with non secular guides and mentors who can provide steerage and records.

In Hinduism, there's also a belief inside the significance of maintaining a balance between the physical and religious worlds. Some believe that using the Ouija board can disrupt this balance and cause horrible effects. Others be given as real with that the board can be used as a device to beautify this balance and assist human beings connect more deeply with the non secular international.

While there can be no single view at the Ouija board in Hinduism, it's miles generally believed that the use of the board calls for warning, recognize, and an know-how of the functionality dangers and blessings worried.

Native American Spirituality:

Native American spirituality varies among tribes, however many have their very private ideals and practices concerning the spirit worldwide and conversation with the vain. Some tribes view the Ouija board as a tool of the satan or a portal for malevolent spirits, whilst others view it as a innocent activity.

One of the principle troubles for Native Americans concerning the Ouija board is the capability for cultural appropriation. Some individuals and businesses have advertised "Native American Ouija boards," that have been criticized as disrespectful and exploitative of indigenous cultures.

www.ingramcontent.com/pod-product-compliance
Lightning Source LLC
Chambersburg PA
CBHW071445080526
44587CB00014B/1996